Introduc

Snowdonia (Eryri) is a beautiful area formed during the Ice Age. At its hea 3,560 ft/1085 metres the highest mountain 19thC the area around Snowdon has attract rock-climbers alike. It is the busiest part of ....uonia National Park, but remains a stronghold of Welsh culture and language. Over the years the natural landscape has been shaped by traditional hill farming and the quarrying for slate and mining for copper. The area has three narrow gauge steam railways: Snowdon Mountain, Llanberis Lake and the Welsh Highland Railway and also the National Slate Museum. The National Trust and the Snowdonia Society play a key role in protecting and enhancing the National Park.

The best way to appreciate the area's stunning scenery and fascinating history is to explore on foot the valleys and lesser known foothills of the high mountain peaks. Apart from a popular climb up Snowdon, this book offers lower level walking routes up to 2,500 feet/760 metres for people of all abilities, visiting places of interest. There are walks by rivers, through woodland and impressive slate quarries, past valley and upland lakes. Some follow waymarked National Trust trails, perhaps in the company of mountain goats. Others offer close views of the steam railways. For the more experienced, there are more demanding lower mountain tops or ridge walks.

The 36 walks in this updated second edition range from an easy 1¼ mile riverside ramble suitable for wheelchairs/pushchairs to a challenging 9½ mile exploration of a rugged remote area of upland lakes. They follow public rights of way and permissive paths or cross Open Access land. A key feature is that many individual routes, as well as containing shorter walk options, can easily be linked with others, to provide longer day walks, if required. Many of the walks are accessible by regular Snowdon Sherpa bus services.

Be properly prepared and equipped for this mountainous area, where weather conditions can quickly change. Walking boots are required, along with provisions, map and appropriate clothing to protect against the elements. Please remember that path conditions can vary according to season and weather, and that even low level paths can be rocky or muddy. Refer any public path problems encountered to Gwynedd Council Rights of Way section (www.gwynedd.gov.uk).

Each walk has a detailed map and description, but bear in mind though that changes in detail can occur at any time. The location of each walk is shown on the back cover and a summary of their key features is also given. This includes an estimated walking time, but allow more time to enjoy the scenery and sights.

Please observe the country code. *Enjoy your walking.*

CWM LLUGWY

DESCRIPTION A 5 mile (**A**) or 4¼ mile (**B**) walk around the attractive wooded Llugwy valley. The route climbs through Coed Bryn Brethynau to a good viewpoint, then passes through more woodland by a choice of track or path, before continuing to Tŷ Hyll (Ugly House), with tea-rooms. It then returns by a quiet country road past the site of Caer Llugwy Roman fort, with Cyfyng falls and Bryn-Glo cafe to finish. Allow about 3 hours

START Bryn-Glo car park SH 736571.

DIRECTIONS The signposted car park adjoins the A5 at the eastern end of Capel Curig.

I Cross the ladder-stile into Coed Bryn Brethynau and follow the narrow stony track up through the trees and past a cottage. A green track then continues up to another cottage. Follow a path towards its outbuilding and up through the wood to a path junction. Turn RIGHT up the path near a wall to cross a ladder-stile over it. Keep ahead then turn RIGHT through a gap in the old wall and follow the signed permissive path up the wide green slope, past waymarker posts and ahead across a field to a ladder-stile/gate at a good viewpoint to join an enclosed public footpath.

2 Follow it RIGHT to cross a ladder-stile and a nearby step stile to join a track, which you follow along the forest edge, past an old track on the left. Just after it bends left you have a choice to point 3. For **Walk B** take a path on the right down through mixed woodland to a footbridge and up to a forestry track, then turn right. For **Walk A** continue down the track, shortly bending north through the forest. After ½ mile at a track junction, bear RIGHT down the wide stony track.

3 When it splits go up the left fork signposted to Tŷ Hyll and Swallow Falls, then take a similarly signed path on the right alongside a wall down to cross a stream and ladder-stile. Keep ahead between boundar-

ies, passing above the nearby house, then alongside the fence. Just before a waymarked gate bend LEFT up through mature trees then turn RIGHT across the stream to a stile. Follow the path along a wood edge, past a cottage and along its access track to join a stony forestry track to reach a minor road. Follow it down to the A5. *Nearby Tŷ Hyll is said to have originally been a 'tŷ unnos' – a house built between sunset and sunrise, which according to ancient law gave ownership to the builder if the chimney emitted smoke from a fire by dawn! It now provides a tea-room and a garden to explore.* Cross the road and with care the bridge over the Afon Llugwy. Turn along the side road – *the former coaching road, before Telford's new 1819 road improvement, now the A5. Follow it past the site of Caer Llugwy Roman fort – built in AD 90 and also known as Bryn-y-Gefeiliau (The Hill of the Metal). Later it passes through Coryn the old quarry hamlet of Pont-Cyfyng. At the A5 turn RIGHT along the pavement above Cyfyng falls back to the start.*

2

WALK 2

CRIMPIAU

DESCRIPTION A 5½ mile walk (**A**) featuring woodland and two craggy hilltops offering great mountain views. The route climbs through Coed Bryn Brethynau, crosses open country, then follows an old packhorse route up to the bwlch beneath Crimpiau. After a choice of routes to its summit (1558 ft/475 metres), it descends past Llyn Coryn to Clogwyn-mawr (1138 ft/347 metres), before returning via Coed Bryn Brethynau. The walk is for experienced hill walkers and should be avoided in poor visibility. Allow about 3½ hours. Included is an easier 2 mile walk (**B**).
START As **Walk I**.

1 Follow instructions in paragraph **1** of **Walk 1**.

2 Turn LEFT to a nearby stile and on to another. The path continues through trees up to a ladder-stile into Open Access land. A waymarked path then descends to a narrow green cross-track. (For **Walk B**, turn left and resume text in paragraph 5.) Follow the surfaced path ahead towards Clogwyn-mawr. Just before the footbridge over Nant y Geuallt, turn RIGHT and follow the waymarked path up to a ladder-stile and on along the attractive

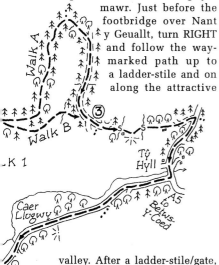

valley. After a ladder-stile/gate, the path crosses Nant y Geuallt then follows it up the narrow valley beneath Crimpiau. At the bwlch the stony path lev-

els out and splits. Take the left fork.

3 Just beyond a boulder turn LEFT along another path and through a wall gap. The path rises towards Crimpiau, shortly near the head of Cwm Crafnant. The path splits – *with a great view back down to Llyn Crafnant*. One option (**b**) is to climb the rocky slope ahead, then follow a path up Crimpiau's N.E. slope and on to its summit. The preferred option (**a**) is to follow the path bending LEFT towards Moel Siabod. Soon the good path rises steadily across the eastern slope, then more steeply to the summit.

4 From the summit follow a path south along the heather covered ridge, soon descending then continuing along the ridge's western edge just below its top. The path then steadily descends to a small plateau and passes Llyn Coryn to reach the left hand corner of the fence ahead. It follows the fence down to a ladder-stile, then descends to cross another. Turn RIGHT between the fence and an old wall, then climb up to the first craggy top of Clogwyn-mawr. Descend south to cross a wall, then follow a path up to the second top. Descend its western slope towards a ladder-stile in the fence below, then follow a path RIGHT round the edge of a reedy area to join the fence. Follow it back to the ladder-stile crossed earlier. Turn RIGHT and follow a path down beneath Clogwyn-mawr's bracken covered slopes, at the bottom bending RIGHT and continuing to cross the footbridge over the river. Follow your outward path to the green track. Turn RIGHT.

5 Go along the track, soon descending to a ladder-stile. At a waymarker post further down, turn LEFT to descend to a ladder-stile into Coed Bryn Brethynau. A delightful path descends then contours through the wood past a side path. Soon after a stone building, turn LEFT up a narrow meandering green track. After passing a telegraph pole and through a wall, turn RIGHT along a path up to a wall-gap and down past a viewpoint to join your outward route below the second cottage.

LLYN Y FOEL

DESCRIPTION A 6½ mile walk, with good views, to a scenic upland lake beneath the majestic Moel Siabod. From Pont Cyfyng the route follows an old track up through woodland and across an expansive open upland area, then a forestry track to the Afon Ystumiau. A path climbs through the forest, then more steeply up to Llyn Foel, at about 1600 ft/490 metres. Paths, wet in places, take you past the lake and beneath Moel Siabod. After following a stony path down past a former slate quarry to a reservoir, the route makes a long steady descent to Pont-Cyfyng. Allow about 4 hours.

START Bryn-Glo car park SH 736571.

DIRECTIONS Travelling from Betws-y-Coed on the A5, the car park is on the right as you enter Capel Curig, with another small parking area on the left just beyond.

I Continue west along the pavement overlooking Cyfyng falls, then cross the early 19th C Pont Cyfyng over the river. Follow the road through the hamlet of Pont-Cyfyng. After ⅓ mile take a signposted path up a stony track on the right past a house and adjoining former chapel up to a ladder-stile/gate. Follow the old stony track up the edge of the wooded valley into open country – *with a first view of Moel Siabod and views looking back to Crimpiau, Craig Wen and the Carneddau*. At a cross-road of tracks keep ahead, soon reaching the track's highest point – *with extensive new views ahead*. The track now crosses expansive moorland/upland pasture to a ladder-stile/gate, then continues to another ladder-stile and enters the forest. Follow the track past two side tracks.

2 At the next track junction by a finger post, turn RIGHT signposted to Moel Siabod. Follow the track through the forest, shortly bending past an old track on the left and rising, then passing a track on the right. Shortly the track enters an area of open mixed woodland – *with Moel Siabod ridge ahead* – and reaches a large turning area, where it splits. Head to a large footbridge,

just beyond a forestry bridge over the Afon Ystumiau. After crossing the bridge turn RIGHT and follow a path up through an area of cleared forest, with the Afon Ystumiau never far away, later briefly near a fence, to a ladder-stile by a waterfall into Open Access land. Follow the path up through heather.

3 When it levels out cross the stream where convenient and follow an improving path, soon rising past a small waterfall. Just above it the path passes to the right of a boulder, then rises steadily up the bracken-covered hillside, with higher falls nearby, soon above a tributary stream which quickly disappears underground. The good path heads up the bracken, heather and stone covered slope. (You are aiming for a V-shaped cleft in the ridge on the skyline.) The path then continues above the right bank of the stream for the final ascent, with a little easy scrambling, to reach Llyn y Foel – *with a good view across the lake to Moel Siabod*. Cross the small stone dam above the lake outlet and follow a path above the heather-covered craggy edge above the lake. Later the path heads away from the lake to reach a cross-path beneath the rocky eastern ridge of Moel Siabod.

4 Turn RIGHT along the path, soon passing round a wet area, and crossing a small rocky ridge. The path continues northwards across occasionally wet/peaty undulating terrain past the lake. It then rises across drier ground, becoming a more distinct stony path as it passes beneath the steep eastern slopes of Moel Siabod. The path then steadily descends to pass a large deep dark quarry pool, and continues down past former quarry buildings and spoil heaps of Rhos quarry. *Slates were taken from the quarry down to Pont Cyfynog, loaded onto carts and carried to Trefriw for transferring to boats. Later it levels out as it passes above a reservoir then continues along the remains of an old track – a former quarry tramway.*

5 After a ladder-stile the track makes a long steady descent – *offering extensive views from the Clwydian Range in the east*

4

to the Glyders and Carneddau in the west – to another ladder-stile/gate. Continue down the track, then a wider stony track to a ladder-stile/gate by Siabod holiday cottages. After a further 50 yards, take the signposted stony path on the right through bracken down to a road. Follow it down to join your outward route in Pont-Cyfyng to reach the A5. *The single storey building opposite, with patterned slate roof is the Rhos quarry's former pay office.*

CAPEL CURIG

Pont-Cyfyng

cafe

Cyfyng Falls

N

0   ¼

mile

S ⑤

reservoir

old quarry workings

Llyn y Foel

Llyn y Foel

Afon Ystumiau

③

②

G

G

5

CAPEL CURIG

DESCRIPTION A 4 mile walk of great variety around Capel Curig, featuring a classic view of Snowdon. The route follows an open bridleway, then crosses the outlet of Llynnau Mymbyr to follow woodland tracks and riverside path to Pont-Cyfyng and nearby waterfalls. It returns past an old coaching inn, passes through woodland, crosses upland pasture then follows an old packhorse trail beneath Clogwyn-mawr, with an optional diversion to Y Pincin for good views. Allow about 2½ hours.

START Capel Curig Snowdonia National Park car park SH 721583.

DIRECTIONS In Capel Curig, at the A5/A4086 junction take the minor road passing the side of Pinnacle Stores, Joe Browns and toilets to reach the car park.

Capel Curig, originally centred around St Julitta's 14thC church – the smallest in Snowdonia – was famous for harp making in the early 17thC. In the late 18thC, Lord Penrhyn built a coach road from Nant Ffrancon to Capel Curig, crossing the Afon Llugwy by the stone bridge of Hen Bont (adjoining the car park). However, the rough road proved to be hazardous to both horses and passengers, and was replaced by a new turnpike road, now the A5, which extended to Betws-y-Coed in 1802. In 1800 Lord Penrhyn built Capel Curig Inn, the first hotel in the area. It was later renamed the Royal Hotel after Queen Victoria stayed there in 1870, and is now part of Plas-y-Brenin, the National Centre for Mountain Activities. After 1808 Capel Curig became an important stopping place on the new Shrewsbury – Holyhead mail coach route, later improved by Thomas Telford, then developed to accommodate an influx of tourists.

I Continue up the road then stony track to cross a ladder-stile. Turn LEFT up a path, then bend LEFT along a narrow green track past the nearby house/outbuilding. Follow the old gated track to the A5. Cross the road and turn LEFT to go through a small gate just before Plas-y-Brenin. Follow the path down – *enjoying a superb view along Llynnau Mymbyr*

to Snowdon – to a footbridge over the lake's outlet and on to a nearby stony forestry track. Follow it LEFT to a stile/gate and on beneath the tree-covered slope to gates by 16thC Bryn Engan. Continue along the track through the mature woodland of Coed Bryn-engan to join another track. Soon take the right fork past a barrier. The stony track narrows to a wide woodland path. After steps a narrow path continues above the river then descends and splits. Take the left fork down to a footbridge leading to nearby Cobden's Hotel on the A5 Descend to the bend of the river just beyond and continue with the wooded riverside path to a ladder-stile into a field.

2 Continue beside the river, through a wall gap, along the next field edge and past a ruined stone barn. Keep by the river, past a telegraph pole and on to cross a footbridge over a stream. Beneath the nearby house turn LEFT up a rough track to join its access track near gates. At the nearby road turn LEFT across the early 19thC Pont Cyfyng to the A5 *Nearby are Cyfyng Falls.* Cross the road and turn LEFT along the pavement to Tyn-y-Coed inn. *The old coach opposite is a reminder of a past era. The inn, with its 17thC back bar was popular with quarrymen from the Rhos quarry below Moel Siabod.* Continue along the pavement.

3 Just before the former school, now the Community Centre, go through its small car park to a ladder-stile into Coed Bryn Brethynau. A stony path meanders up through trees to a cross path. Follow it LEFT through the predominantly oak woodland shortly rising to a ladder-stile at its edge. Go up to a waymarker post at a prominent view point and to another at a green track. Follow the waymarked path through a wall gap ahead and on to a ladder-stile. Continue near the fence, passing above a wooden chalet, to join its access track by a telephone mast. On the bend follow the signed path through the gate ahead.

4 Just beyond, turn RIGHT alongside the fence to a ladder-stile/gate. Follow the path through trees into Open Access land crossing two streams, then the more substantive Nant y Geuallt. The path continues towards a large footbridge over the river. Just before it turn sharp LEFT along a wide stony path – *the old packhorse trail between Llanrwst and Capel* – to a gate/ladder-stile and on through woodland to leave it by another gate/ladder-stile. After crossing a stream you have a choice. You can simply continue on the main path. Alternatively, to enjoy good views from the nearby small hillock of Y Pincin, turn LEFT to the bottom of a rocky slope. Follow a path through bracken up to boulders and rock slabs, then climb up to a final slab on Y Pincin. Return back down, then bear RIGHT between rock slabs and down to a wall/fence. Turn RIGHT down to rejoin the main path at a gateway. Follow it down to the road junction by St Curig's church – *built in 1880 to cater for the summer visitors. Nearby is a former turnpike cottage.* Cross the road with care to the Pinnacle Café, which makes a good finish.

Follow the wide path up the field to an old gateway, then a path across the nearby stream and continue east towards Clogwyn-mawr past Y Pincin to a ladder-stile/gate. Continue through woodland and on to another ladder-stile/gate. Follow the wide stony path ahead. Just before a large footbridge over the river, turn LEFT and follow a path towards high ground. It then skirts the lower slopes of Clogwyn-mawr, before rising, later more steeply to a ladder-stile. Turn LEFT between the old wall and a fence. At the wall corner climb to the first craggy top Descend south, cross a wall, then climb to the second top.

2 Descend its western slope to a ladder-stile in the fence below. (From here, to main-

WALK 5
CLOGWYN-MAWR

DESCRIPTION A short but rewarding 2 mile walk, featuring an energetic climb up Clogwyn-mawr (1138 feet/347 metres) offering panoramic mountain views. *Avoid in poor visibility.* Allow about 2 hours.
START As Walk 4.

1 Return to the junction. Cross the A5 and a ladder-stile opposite near a war memorial.

tain the views to Snowdon, you can work your way on intermittent paths across the gorse and heather-covered hillside, in a gradual descent to a fence and a gate as shown.)
The path continues down to another ladder-stile, then descends the steep bracken covered

WALK 6

TAL-Y-BRAICH

DESCRIPTION A 7½ mile (**A**) or 7 mile (**B**) walk exploring the expansive wild upper Llugwy valley, enclosed by mountains. The route follows a former 18thC coach road (See Walk 4) for nearly 2½ miles along the valley's south side, then a bridleway through National Trust owned Tal-y-Braich. A choice of routes climb to join a leat, contouring across the hillside at around 1370 ft/420 metres to a viewpoint overlooking Llyn Cowlyd, which it serves. There follows a long steady descent to the A5. Allow about 4½ hours.

START Capel Curig Snowdonia National Park car park SH 721583. See Walk 4.

I Continue up the road. At its end by a house, go to a ladder-stile/gate ahead. Go along the part stony track, later bending west along Cwm Llugwy. After a ladder-stile/gate the track continues unerringly straight to gates into National Trust owned Glyderau land, then passes beneath the northern slopes of Gallt yr Ogof – *shortly with a good view of Tryfan*. At Scots Pines cross a ladder-stile by an old iron gate and follow the path across the Afon Llugwy to the A5. Go along the stony track opposite into Tal-y-braich. Follow it up to the rear of outbuildings. Just beyond follow the well waymarked bridleway up past a cottage to a stile/gate. Follow the bridleway east above the wall, shortly passing a stone building. Follow the wall down to a part stony cross track at a gate in it. (For **Walk B** continue ahead down the bridleway to a small gate and across a delightful stone slab bridge. Turn left along the reedy bank. After 25 yards the bridleway gradually moves away from the stream, briefly rejoins it, then rises across the moorland to rejoin Walk A at the leat.)

2 Turn LEFT up the track towards Cwm Tal-y-braich, through a gate, and on up to contour just beneath an embankment hiding the leat. Near the bend of the leat the track descends to cross a stream. Continue up to a small bridge across the leat. Now follow the stiled path on the embankment above the leat, past another bridge, then an old sluice gate. At the next bridge you are joined by Walk B. Continue along the leat path, past two further bridges, after which the leat bends towards Creigiau Gleision. Just before the next enclosed bridge, cross a small footbridge over another narrow leat. At a cross-path beyond turn LEFT to cross the bridge and stile, then follow the leat for 100 yards to its final bridge, from where water tumbles into Llyn Cowlyd. Return to cross the bridge.

3 Follow the path near the fence through heather to cross a footbridge over the narrow leat. The path now begins a long steady descent south across moorland to a ladder-stile/gate. Continue with the path, soon taking its left fork down to cross a stream. After passing above a house, keep ahead to follow the path on a long steady descent through bracken to a ladder-stile onto the A5. Cross it with care and follow the stony roadside path to Capel Curig.

WALK 7

GALLT Y OGOF

DESCRIPTION A 5½ mile walk and climb (**A**) to Gallt y Ogof (2,503 ft/763 metres), a foothill of the Glyders, or easier 4 mile walk (**B**), both offering extensive mountain views. From Cwm Llugwy, the route heads across open ground to join the ridge at 1673 ft/510 metres leading to Gallt y Ogof. After a steep ascent to its summit, Walk A then returns with Walk B across the wide moorland ridge and down rocky Cregiau r Gelli. Allow about 4 and 3 hours respectively. For experienced hill walkers. Avoid in poor visibility.

I Continue up the road. At its end by a house, go to a ladder-stile/gate ahead. Go along the part stony track, later bending west along the expansive Cwm Llugwy. About 15 yards beyond a ladder-stile/gate, turn LEFT along a path through reeds to a nearby stream. Angle slightly RIGHT (SW) across open ground aiming for where a wall kinks

8

on the distant ridge leading to Gallt y Ogof. Intermittent paths take you to just below the wall as shown. Follow the wall, later rising more steeply and bending. At the wall/ fence corner cross a stile to reach a ladder-stile beyond – *with views to Moel Siabod and Lliwedd.* (For **Walk B** resume text in paragraph 3.)

Cwm Tal·y·braich

Llyn Cowlyd

leat

WALK A

WALK B

leat

leat

3

Upland leat

2

WALK 6

A5

Afon Llugwy

wall

N

Gallt yr Ogof

WALK 7

0   ¼
mile

Cregiau'r Gelli

Cefn y Capel

2 3

Bwlch Goleuni

1 P

CAPEL CURIG

A4086

2 Follow the path up the steep slope, soon alongside an old wall. At its corner, keep ahead, then follow a minor path up alongside the fence – *later with a view to Llyn Cowlyd.* Just below the top fence corner, bear LEFT up the green slope to a tiny pool between the two rocky tops of Gallt y Ogof. Climb the one to your left to reach its summit cairn to enjoy all-round views. Descend its southern slope to join a cross-path. Follow it LEFT, soon descending to rejoin the fence and continue down to the ladder-stile.

3 Cross the ladder-stile and follow the path down and across the wide wettish moor-land of Bwlch Goleuni to another ladder-stile, and on across the south-facing slope of Cefn y Capel. The path briefly descends towards Capel Curig, then bears LEFT (NE) along a shelf. As it begins to descend, it bears RIGHT (E) down a wide gully, crosses an old wall, and continues down past a large rock slab. It then angles to the left down the rocky slope of Cregiau r Gelli to reach the green track by the house. Keep ahead to join your outward route.

CARNEDD Y CRIBAU

DESCRIPTION A 6 mile walk for experienced hill walkers, featuring a splendid rocky ridge offering panoramic mountain views. The initial section crosses expansive wettish moorland on intermittent paths, then climbs to the small crag of Cefnycerrig. After diverting to Clogwyn Bwlch y maen for new views, the route climbs to Carnedd y Cribau (1938 ft/590 metres) and follows the ridge path/ fence on a long steady descent to Bwlch y Rhediad. After descending into Nant Gwynant it returns along a section of the old valley road. Allow 4½ – 5 hours. Avoid in poor visibility.

START Near A498/A4086 junction SH 659555.

DIRECTIONS There is pay & display roadside parking on both sides of the A498 just south of Pen-y-Gwryd Hotel and the A4086.

I From the southern end of the parking area on the east side cross a ladder-stile by a gate. Take a faint but improving path angling slightly RIGHT up the slope. It then bends half-LEFT up across higher ground. After about 50 yards, the main path bears RIGHT. When it bends left keep ahead up the stone-covered slope to pass to the left of a prominent rock on the skyline, where the ground levels out. Keep ahead for another 60 yards to the edge of wet moorland. Here turn LEFT and follow a sketchy path east. Cross a small rise and continue to a distinctive rock ahead (**A**). Follow a path half-RIGHT to a small rocky knoll (**B**).

2 From its top continue south east. Work your way round wet/ peaty areas to reach a large solitary boulder (**C**). Go across another wet area to cross Nant-y-llys, then follow the clear path up the slope ahead. After a wet area, continue up the part rocky slope, soon on a clear path. When it fades angle RIGHT up to pass between small crags, from where a path climbs steadily to a ladder-stile in a fence beneath Cefnycerrig. Cross the stile and climb to its craggy summit. Descend its southern slope, then go past a small pool, and up to the fence corner. Continue alongside the fence, past two ladder-stiles and up to the top of nearby Clogwyn Bwlch y maen. Return to cross the ladder-stile giving access to the ridge path. Follow the fence up to cross adjoining ladder-stiles to reach the summit of Carnedd y Cribau.

The Pen-y-Gwryd Hotel has been popular with climbers and walkers for over 200 years. The team which climbed Everest in 1953 stayed here whilst training in Snowdonia.

10

3 After crossing a nearby ladder-stile, continue on a path beside the fence, passing two ladder-stiles. The path now descends in stages, occasionally looping away from the fence, first to avoid a steep crag, then wet areas. After a descent section the fence briefly bends away from the path and old fence posts. When the fence then begins a steep descent, go up the high ground ahead by the old iron posts, then descend steeply beneath crags following the old posts to rejoin the fence. Follow it down to a ladder-stile at Bwlch y Rhediad.

4 Turn RIGHT and follow a bridleway towards Snowdon, soon descending – *with Llyn Gwynant below* – to a ladder-stile/gate. The bridleway descends steadily across the stone/bracken covered slope, later more steeply through woodland to eventually reach the A498. Cross the road to a nearby ladder-stile/gate. Descend the steep slope and through trees to a minor road. Follow it north up the valley past Gwastadanas to its end at a bridge over a stream. Continue up a stony track ahead to eventually reach the A498 near the start.

WALK 9

SNOWDON

DESCRIPTION A demanding 7¼ mile walk **(A)** for experienced hill walkers to the top of Snowdon and an alternative 5½ mile walk **(B)**, combining two popular approaches to Snowdon from the high start of Pen-y-Pass (1178 ft)/359 metres), featuring three lakes set amidst superb mountain scenery. The route follows the Miners' Track, built to serve 19th C Brittania copper mine, to Glaslyn lake (1985 ft/605 metres). After a short steep climb to 2460 ft/750 metres, Walk B returns early along the high level, but rougher rocky Pyg Track. Walk A first continues up to Snowdon summit. Allow about 5 and 4 hrs respectively. For an enjoyable 6 mile walk on Snowdon without the hard climbing, simply follow the Miners' Track to Glaslyn and back. Keep to the main paths and avoid in poor visibility. Be properly dressed and equipped. The car park quickly fills, so use the frequent Sherpa bus service from Nant Peris, or walk the new link path from Pen y Gwryd. There is a café and bus waiting room.
START Pen-y-Pass car park SH 647556.

1 From the lower car park, follow the Miners' Track to pass above Llyn Teyrn, then over the causeway built across Llyn Llydaw in 1853, and on alongside the lake. After passing the former copper crushing mill, a stone path climbs steadily to Glaslyn. Just past ruined barracks, follow the stone path up the rocky hillside.

2 A large vertical stone marks the junction with the Pyg Track. (For **Walk B** turn RIGHT and follow the stony Pyg path across the mountainside to eventually cross a ladder-stile by the waymarked path to Grib Goch. The path now begins its final long steady descent to Pen y Pass.) From here the path climbs steadily, later zigzagging up the route originally used by mules to carry copper from the mine to another large marker stone on the main ridge. Follow the railway

line up to the summit. Return down to point 2, then follow the Pyg Track (Walk B) or the easier Miners' Track.

LLYN GWYNANT & CWM GLASLYN

DESCRIPTION A 5 mile figure of eight walk (**A**) combining a circuit of Llyn Gwynant with an exploration of an attractive enclosed valley beneath the Snowdon range, featuring the early 20th C Cwm-Dyli power station, or a 2¾ mile walk around Llyn Gwynant (**B**). Allow about 3½ and 2½ hours respectively
START Roadside parking near the northern end of Llyn Gwynant SH 648518.

I Follow the roadside path north-east, then instructions in paragraph 3 of Walk 11 to the ladder-stile in the penultimate sentence. For **Walk A** now follow instructions in paragraph 2 below. (For **Walk B** continue to cross the stone slab footbridge, then follow instructions in paragraphs 4 of Walk 11 to the A498, then return on the pavement along the southern side of the lake.)

2 Cross the ladder-stile/sleeper bridge to a small gate. Go along the long field to cross a stile in its right-hand corner, a stream and a ladder-stile beyond. Follow the edge of the large reedy field to a stile onto a minor road. Follow it north along the valley, later passing Gwastadanas, to its end at a bridge over a fast flowing stream. (Here a small gate on the left provides a shorter option as shown.) Just beyond go down the left of two stony tracks – *with the Afon Glaslyn tumbling down the hillside ahead* – to the gated entrance of Cwm-Dyli power station by the river. Keep ahead. *This attractive utilitarian building (1906), linked by water pipes descending from Llyn Llydaw, once provided local hillside quarries with power. A wooden*

shack was a mess hall and social centre for the workforce employed here.

3 At the end of the track go through a small gate ahead by a corrugated building, cross a stone slab bridge over the river and follow the fence round to cross a bridge over the pipeline and a ladder-stile. Follow the path to cross a facing ladder-stile, then through a long reedy field. Continue with a stonier path, flirting with the river, to eventually reach the stone slab bridge over the river, where you join Walk B to complete the circuit of Llyn Gwynant (see paragraph 1 above).

Llyn Gwynant

12

NANT GWYNANT
&
LLYN GWYNANT

DESCRIPTION A delightful 6¼ mile (**A**) or 4½ mile (**B**) walk, featuring woodland, upland pasture, and the beautiful Llyn Gwynant. Walk B returns along the lake's southern side. Walk A returns above its northern side. A visit to nearby Gwynant cafe afterwards is recommended. Allow about 4 and 3 hours respectively.
START Pont Bethania car park, Nant Gwynant SH 628507. See Walk 13.

I From the car park's northern end, take the signposted path along the driveway from Plas Gwynant lodge. Just past a cottage, follow the waymarked path up a stony track, then lane, passing above Plas Gwynant. At a cattle-grid, turn RIGHT down the waymarked path, over the river and on up to join a minor road. It rises steadily. After just over ½ mile, on the bend, go through a small gate on the left by a finger post. Follow the path to gates and on by the river to cross a footbridge over it. Follow the path across reedy ground, past a nearby house, through a wall gap and on across upland pasture – *enjoying good views of the Snowdon range* – to a small gate in a wall corner.

2 The initially boardwalked path continues through rhododendrons to a ladder-stile into Nant Gwynant. Follow the path through the forest, midway crossing a stream and ladder-stile. Eventually, at a wall corner, the path bends left briefly along the wood edge, then right to pass a stone barn. Ignore the cross-path and follow an improving path ahead across reedy ground, then down beside a wall. Just before a facing wall bear RIGHT along a faint green track, then go down an old walled stony track towards Llyn Gwynant. When it bends left, follow a path ahead down past the bend of a track, then down near a wall to join the stony track, which descends to the A498. Cross to the pavement opposite. (For **Walk B** turn left alongside the lake to rejoin the main route at point 5). Turn RIGHT

and continue along the roadside path beside the lake.

3 After passing a ladder-stile/gate on the right, angle LEFT past an information board and on beside the lake to ladder-stile. Continue with the lakeside path, shortly rising across a gorse covered knoll, then descending to a small gate. Follow the path to a seat, then go along the shore. Where a piped stream enters the lake, turn RIGHT to reach a cross-track in Gwynant campsite. Go along another track ahead, through a gateway, past a side track, then keep ahead along the field edge to a ladder-stile. Turn LEFT to cross a delightful stone slab footbridge over the river.

4 Follow a path southwestwards near the river beneath the rock debris covered slope to a small gate and on beneath the steep slopes to a ladder-stile. The path now rises through a wood, past a viewpoint over the lake, then crosses the part wooded slope. After a stream, it bends left. Ignore a descending path, but follow a path up through the trees to a delightful crag overlooking the lake – *a good stopping place*. Continue through trees, soon taking the higher path up across a small rocky ridge. The path then descends through the trees and levels out. Take the right fork round the tree-topped knoll to a ladder-stile. The path continues up a part reedy valley, shortly levelling out before descending past old mine workings to a wall gap. After crossing a stream just beyond, turn LEFT towards a house. Turn RIGHT along its stony access track, shortly near the river. Just before a ladder-stile/gate by Ysgubor Bwlch, continue beside the river to cross an old stone slab footbridge over it to a gate into a field. Follow the path's right fork round to a ladder-stile and up to the A498.

5 Turn RIGHT and follow the pavement through the hamlet of Nantgwynant. Later take a signposted path up a narrow driveway on the left to Snowdon View. (Or continue along the pavement, then grass verge.) Go past the cottage and follow the path through the trees down to the lane near Plas Gwynant. Return along your outward route. *The nearby Gwynant café makes a rewarding end to the walk.*

MOEL MEIRCH & LLYN EDNO

DESCRIPTION An exhilarating 9½ mile exploration of a delightful wild undulating rugged upland area of many small lakes and rocky crags, mainly on paths, offering panoramic mountain views. The route climbs to Moel Meirch (1991 ft/607 metres), passes the scenic Llyn Edno, then continues generally south past smaller lakes, reaching a height of 2132 ft/650 metres. It then heads west to Llyn yr Adar, before a dramatic descent to pass near Llyn Llagi, followed by a steadier descent in stages. Allow about 6 hours. *For experienced hill walkers only and should be avoided in poor visibility, when you can easily become disorientated.*
START Pont Bethania car park, Nant Gwynant SH 628507. (See Walk 13) or old road just south of Gwynant café.

I From the car park's northern end, take the signposted path along the driveway from Plas Gwynant lodge. Just past a cottage, follow the waymarked path up a stony track, then lane, passing above Plas Gwynant. At a cattle-grid, turn RIGHT down the waymarked path, over the river and on up to join a minor road. It rises steadily. After just over ½ mile, on the bend take the signposted path (Edno) down a stony track ahead. It soon bends left to a ladder-stile/gate and continues up to another ladder-stile. Just beyond, when the track bends to a house, go through a gate ahead. Follow the path to a gate, cross two streams, then follow a reedy path to another gate in a boundary corner. The path rises to a further gate – *with good views to Snowdon* – then up through a wall gap below old buildings. Bear LEFT through reeds onto a small rise by two trees, then continue across upland pasture, over an old wall and stream by a small tree, to cross a ladder-stile ahead.

2 Turn LEFT on a path beside the wall, soon rising to pass through three wall-gaps beneath crags. Continue along the right

bank of the Afon Llynedno up the attractive boulder strewn valley, past small waterfalls. The valley later widens, where the path moves away from the stream across wettish ground past a tiny stone enclosure, following the stream's main right fork. After rejoining the stream, continue beside it for about 25 yards to a small hawthorn tree just before the stream is enclosed by crags. Here, go half-RIGHT up the slope, then across its small level top for about 12 yards to reach a clear cross-path. Follow it up, passing behind the large crag overlooking the stream, then along the left-hand side of a small reedy gully to climb onto the high ground, soon with a view down to the stream.

3 The path climbs onto the facing crag and continues along the wide valley, soon near the stream. After passing a sheepfold, it crosses two side streams, then the Afon Llynedno. The path continues up the narrowing valley edge, soon rising steadily beneath heather covered slopes to your right, to eventually reach the bwlch between two crags, with Llyn Edno glimpsed to your right. Turn LEFT and follow a meandering path across undulating ground to the summit of Moel Meirch to enjoy all-round mountain views. Retrace your steps and continue to Llyn Edno.

4 From small crags at the end of the lake, continue parallel to the nearby fence, soon guided by old iron fence posts and rising across the undulating boulder covered terrain. Later the path leaves the posts to pass to the right of high ground, before rejoining the fence. After climbing up Ysgafell Wen the path continues south along the ridge to pass close to one of the Llynnau 'r Cwn group of lakes. Follow the fence up to pass a tiny pool on your left, then climb up to the top of the nearby crag - the highest point of the walk - enjoying extensive views of three more lakes, Cnicht, the Moelwyns and Cardigan Bay. Descend to rejoin the fence, shortly passing another small lake, then a ladder-stile and gate in the fence.

Continue up beside the fence to reach a small pool at its corner. Keep beside the fence for a further 200 yards, gently descending - with a new lake visible ahead.

5 At small crags where the fence bends and descends steeply, turn sharp RIGHT on a side path heading west along the edge of a small plateau. It passes a small pool and

on down to join a cross-path. It descends past quarry waste, crosses an old low wall, and descends to a small stone ruin. The path now descends in stages to a ladder-

goes along a rocky ridge towards Cnicht, passing above another lake, before making a gradual descent towards Llyn yr Adar. It passes a path angling off to the right, later passing two more side paths on the right and a small crag on the left, As the path begins to climb towards the slope leading to Cnicht, take the next path on the right. It descends gently towards Llyn yr Adar, later passing above the lake and crossing two streams. It then bends round the end of the lake. After crossing another stream, angle away from the lake across wettish ground to follow a path round beneath small crags, then rising to a good viewpoint of Snowdon. The path descends, soon overlooking Llyn Llagi, briefly climbs, then descends again across steep slopes to a small cairn at the head of the valley.

6 Follow a path down towards the lake, soon leaving the stream to descend the steep mid-slopes, through a wall-gap, and

stile, then makes a long steady descent near a stream to another ladder-stile by a small waterfall. Continue down past a cottage, at its corner turning LEFT to a ladder-stile. Follow the path to another cottage, then go up the slope ahead to a gate onto a minor road. Take the signposted path through a gate opposite by Blaen Nant. Continue beside the wall, then at a ladder-stile angle LEFT up past a telegraph pole onto a small ridge. Turn LEFT briefly along it, then RIGHT down a path. Follow a wall up to cross a ladder-stile. Turn LEFT and follow the wall up across higher ground and down to a narrow track. Follow it RIGHT to eventually reach your outward road.

WALK 13

HAFOD Y LLAN

DESCRIPTION A 2½ mile waymarked trail around Hafod y Llan Farm, featuring riverside and woodland walking. Hafod y Llan estate, with its 17thC farm, includes part of Snowdon and was purchased by public subscription in 1998. It is managed by the National Trust as a traditional organic farm. Allow about 1½ hours. A visit to nearby Gwynant cafe afterwards is recommended.
START Pont Bethania car park, Nant Gwynant SH 628507.
DIRECTIONS The car park lies on the A498 between Llyn Gwynant and Llyn Dinas, about 3 miles north-east of Beddgelert.

From the toilets follow the road over the river, then a path to the A498. Cross to the minor road opposite into Hafod y Llan estate. Go along the road, then take the signposted farm trail over a footbridge on the right and along the riverbank for ½ mile to cross a footbridge at a meeting of rivers. Turn LEFT, then RIGHT on the waymarked red arrow trail, through a wall gap, then along a field edge, initially by the river, to a gateway. Continue ahead along a stony track and through another gateway.

2 Just before a ladder-stile/gate follow the trail LEFT past a stone building and up near the wall. Go through a gap in the corner and turn LEFT along a path, soon bearing RIGHT and continuing between walls up to the large boundary wall of woodland. Turn LEFT and follow the trail between walls down to a small gate, then on beneath the woodland past small ruins. At the wall corner turn LEFT to cross a footbridge over the river. *Upstream is a power house for a new National Trust hydro electric scheme.* Keep ahead briefly then turn RIGHT to a gate into Hafod y Llan campsite. Go up the field edge to the wall end near the river to go through a gate beyond. Cross the stream and turn RIGHT up the field edge to a gate. Go up the stony path, initially above the river, to join the Watkin Path. Turn LEFT and follow the wide stony path down to a gate. Go

through another gate opposite and follow the Watkin Path past an information board and on through the wood down to the A498.

WALK 14

CWM LLAN

DESCRIPTION A 4 mile walk exploring an awe-inspiring enclosed upland valley beneath Snowdon. The route follows the delightful lower section of the Watkin Path to Snowdon through attractive woodland, then up past waterfalls into the dramatic setting of Cwm Llan containing famous Gladstone Rock, and the substantial remains of the former 19thC South Snowdon slate quarry, at just over 1000 ft/300 metres. It returns along an old tramway, descends back into the valley, later diverting to a delightful stone slab bridge by waterfalls. Allow about 2½ hours. An alternative 5 mile walk involves following the Hafod y Llan farm trail to join the Watkin Path higher up. A visit to nearby Gwynant cafe afterwards is recommended.
START As Walk 13.

The Watkin Path is named after Sir Edward Watkin, a Victorian railway tycoon and Liberal MP. who retired to the valley and who had the path constructed. The track, which was originally used by horse-drawn carriage as far as the old quarry, was open to the public in 1892 by the liberal Prime Minister William Gladstone, then 83. He addressed a crowd of over 2000 people at a huge boulder alongside the route, now known as Gladstone rock.

From the toilets follow the road over the river, then a path to the A498. Cross to the minor road opposite and take the signed Watkin Path from a small gate up through the wood to a small gate, and on past the site of Sir Edward Watkin's summer chalet and an information board to a large iron gate onto the original Watkin Path. Go through the gate ahead and follow the wide stony path as it winds its way up the hillside, later passing an old incline to gates into Yr Wyddfa National Nature Reserve. The path continues up above the Afon Cwm Llan

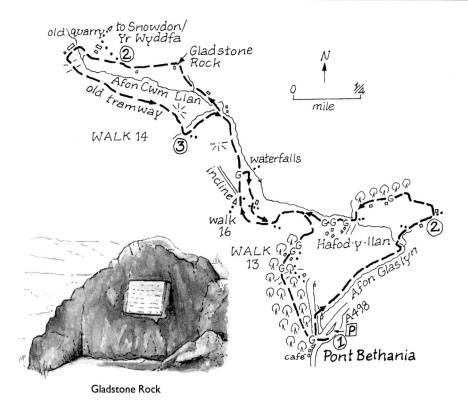

Gladstone Rock

and a series of small waterfalls. After passing the top falls by the former crushing mill for the Hafod-y-Llan copper mines high up on Y Lliwedd, the path levels out by a weir built for the National Trust's hydro-electric scheme. The wide path crosses the river and continues along Cwm Llan past slate fences, with the Snowdon ridge ahead. After passing the ruin of Plas Cwm Llan – *once the South Snowdon Slate Quarry manager's house* – the path continues up the valley past a small crag with a plaque - Gladstone rock – *with the old tramway visible on Yr Aran.*

2 About 120 yards before the remains of South Snowdon slate quarry ahead angle LEFT off the Watkin Path along a wide level green path. It passes beneath the buildings and waste tips to reach a lower part of the slate quarry. After crossing a bridge over the river go past the long ruined building, then the right hand side of a slate 'graveyard'.

Now bend along the old tramway and follow it along the slopes of Yr Aran. *The well constructed tramway carried slate from the quarry via inclines, to the road at Pont Bethania, from where it was taken by horse drawn cart to Porthmadog for loading onto ships.*

3 Later, take a substantial path back down into the valley – *high up on Y Lliwedd ahead are the remains of 17thC copper mines* – then return down the Watkin Path. After the gates, descend a path to a delightful stone slab bridge by waterfalls and pools – *a great place to linger.* Return a few yards then take a path on the left down through bracken and on by a wall to pass a ruin. At a crossroad of paths, keep ahead to the bottom of the old incline, then follow the former tramway to rejoin the Watkin Path. After the gate, either continue on the woodland path or go down the enclosed stony path, then along the minor road to the A498.

17

CRAFLWYN

DESCRIPTION A 1½ mile walk, linking sections of National Trust waymarked trails, rising through the attractive woodland of Coed Craflwyn and across upland pasture grazed by wild goats, with panoramic views. About 600 feet of climbing , steep in places, but well worth the effort. Allow about 1¾ hours.
START Craflwyn National Trust car park SH 600490.
DIRECTIONS Craflwyn lies just off the A498 about 1 mile from Beddgelert.

I From the information board at the rear of the Warden's office go through a small gateway into Coed Craflwyn, then follow the meandering green trail up past a ruin. At a waymarked path junction just beyond a stream, turn LEFT to continue with the green trail up through the wood, past your yellow return path and through a wall gap. It then rises more steeply to another wall gap, recrosses the stream and continues up to a waymarked green/red trail junction at the wood edge. Follow the green trail LEFT through a nearby wall gap and across the open hillside, soon rising near a wall. Beyond its corner, the path does a sharp U-turn back up to a small gateway in the wall and continues up beside it. When the path levels out divert RIGHT to a great viewpoint. Continue with the green trail to a wall gap and on across the hillside to cross a wall. Just beyond turn LEFT, now on the red trail, to a nearby small gate by a ruin, and on across the hillside to a ladder-stile. The path now rises gently then descends to a wall gap.

2 At the next red/black trail waymarker post take the red trail down to a stile. It continues down to pass a large wooden seat at a prominent viewpoint. Later, after a wall gap, the path descends more steeply through trees and another wall gap, then continues down past a side path. At another waymarked path junction, keep ahead to follow the yellow woodland trail through two wall gaps and a stone sheepfold to a small gate, then down to join your outward route.

NANT GWYNANT

DESCRIPTION A varied 7 mile upland and valley walk, with a cafe mid-way. The route follows waymarked National Trust paths up through Coed Craflwyn and across the lower southern slopes of Yr Aran, up through old mine workings to a height of 1115 ft/340 metres, then through a hidden upland valley and down to join the Watkin Path. After descending to Pont Bethania and Gwynant cafe the route returns past Llyn Dinas, then follows the river past Sygun Copper Mine. Allow about 4½ hours.
START Craflwyn National Trust car park. SH 600490 or Pont Bethania SH 628507.

I Follow instructions in paragraph 1 of Walk 15.

2 At the next waymarker post continue ahead on the black waymarked path. After a ladder-stile, continue with the path, soon parallel with a fence. It then bends left through an old wall, and briefly continues beside it, before moving away and gradually descending to pass to the left of a fence corner. The waymarked path continues to a ladder-stile/gate in the fence by a ruin. Cross a stream ahead and a ladder-stile by a gate on the green track above. Follow the former mine track towards Yr Aran. After a gate it rises steadily, initially near the stream, then becomes a green path.

3 After passing a ruined mine building on the left, the path bends RIGHT up to a stream and continues up a narrow rocky valley, past a waste tip and over a steam. The path briefly levels out then rises onto a narrow ridge ahead – *the highest point of the walk, offering new views of Cwm Gorsen below, Cnicht and Moel Siabod*. Descend to a ladder-stile below. The waymarked path continues down into and across the edge of the wide valley, later descending – *with a view ahead of Llyn Gwynant* – then continuing down by a wall – *with Y Lliwedd towering above* – to cross a ladder-stile over it. A wide path now angles LEFT down the hillside to eventually join the wide stony

Watkin Path below an old incline. Follow it down the hillside to go through a large gate and another ahead, then descend the path through woodland to the A498 at Pont Bethania. Turn RIGHT.

4 Go past houses to Gwynant cafe and on along the old road, then take the single track road opposite over the river. On the bend, go along the access track to Llyndy Isaf. Go past the house and outbuildings to a ladder-stile/gate. Follow the path round to a small gate and along the wood edge to a ladder-stile. The path

continues along the edge of expansive tussocky reedy ground adjoining Llyn Dinas to a ladder-stile/gate then past woodland and a ladder-stile. After a stream the path rises to a ladder-stile, continues up through trees, then descends to a ladder-stile by Llyn Dinas. Continue along the path to a kissing gate at the end of the lake. Go past a large footbridge, and follow a path, initially near the river, to a road leading to Sygun Copper Mine.

5 Turn RIGHT to cross the bridge over the river to the A498. Go through a small gate on the left and follow the bridged National Trust path near the river to a gate onto the A498. Cross to a nearby gate into Craflwyn. Go up the driveway, soon bending past the front of the hall, and continuing to the car park.

WALK 17
LLYN DINAS

DESCRIPTION A delightful 3¼ mile linear lake and riverside valley walk from Pont Bethania to Beddgelert, passing the beautiful Llyn Dinas. Allow about 2 hours.
START Pont Bethania SH 628507.
DIRECTIONS Take the Sherpa S97 bus from Beddgelert to Pont Bethania car park on the A498.

Walk back to the entrance to Hafod y Llan estate/Watkin Path, then follow the instructions in Paragraph 4 of Walk 16. Go up Sygun's road and just beyond the car park entrance, turn RIGHT along a waymarked path beside a wall, past a house to join a minor road. (Now see Walk 18 map.) Follow it for about ½ mile. Just before it crosses the river to the A498 go through a kissing gate and follow the riverside path to a footbridge over the river into Beddgelert.

CWM BYCHAN & ABERGLASLYN

DESCRIPTION A 7 mile (**A**), 6 mile (**B**), or 5¾ mile (**C**) walk exploring the hidden upland valley of Cwm Bychan, which was mined for copper from the late 18thC until 1930, the heather-covered hills above Beddgelert, and the beautiful Aberglaslyn Pass. The route rises steadily from Llyn Dinas to the top of Grib Ddu. Walks B and C go more directly into Cwm Bychan, whilst Walk A first follows an undulating heather ridge to the summit of Mynydd Sygun (984 ft/300 metres). After descending to Nantmor, the route passes through woodland, then follows the river along Aberglaslyn Pass, near the Welsh Highland Railway and on to Beddgelert. It then continues via Sygun Copper Mine (café) to Llyn Dinas. Allow about 4½ hours. Avoid in poor visibility. There are other start options.

START Car park near Llyn Dinas SH 612494.

DIRECTIONS The A488 roadside car park is just before Llyn Dinas, 1½ miles from Beddgelert. Alternative parking nearby.

1 Go through a small gate on the south side of the road near Llyn Dinas. Follow the path briefly along the lakeside, then by the river to cross a footbridge over it. Turn LEFT to a kissing gate into National Trust owned Llyndy Isaf near the lake. A few yards beyond, take a stony path on the right up the bracken-covered hillside – *offering a good view along Llyn Dinas*. Eventually it levels out then begins a long steady ascent across the heather-covered enclosed upland valley to a finger post at the top of Grib Ddu. (For **Walk C**, turn left, signposted to Aberglaslyn, to a ladder-stile and follow the path down into Cwm Bychan to point 4.)

2 Keep ahead, signposted to Beddgelert/ Sygun, passing through an old mine to cross a ladder-stile to reach a good viewpoint just beyond. Return to the ladder-stile, then turn RIGHT up a path by the fence. At its corner turn RIGHT to follow an initially stony path down to a junction of paths

by a large boulder in a flat area at Bwlch-y-Sygyn. (For **Walk B** take the path leading left, soon descending past a pool (dry in summer) then a heather-covered hillock to join Walk C descending Cwm Bychan.) For **Walk A** turn RIGHT to a good viewpoint overlooking the valley and across to Snowdon. The path now descends.

3 After about 10 yards, turn LEFT along a path to a nearby finger post (Beddgelert). and on beneath the undulating heather-covered ridge to a pile of stones at a crossroad of paths. Follow the path ahead along the eastern side of the ridge, shortly passing a nearby large cairn and two small pools. Follow a choice of paths, soon merging into a good green path, to begin a steady ascent to the highest point of Mynydd Sygun. Retrace your steps. About 20 yards beyond the large cairn, turn RIGHT down another path. When it splits just before a tiny stone sheepfold, go down the right fork to a path junction. Turn RIGHT and follow the path on a steady descent past a rising path on the left. After levelling out it continues past old mine workings and beneath crags to enter Cwm Bychan. Bear RIGHT.

4 Go past the remains of an aerial ropeway – *that once carried ore down from the nearby mine* – and continue down the valley. After a small gate the path descends through woodland to the National Trust car park and toilets at Nantmor. Follow the signed path to Pont Aberglaslyn through woodland, then continue north along a path above the river through the Aberglaslyn Pass, shortly beneath the West Highland railway. After crossing it, continue beside the river to a footbridge at Beddgelert.

5 Follow the riverside path past a road bridge, through a small gate and on to a kissing gate onto a minor road. Follow it for just over ½ mile. At a finger post at the far end of a wood, either follow the road to Sygun Copper Mine for a visit or refreshments, or take a path ahead beside the wall through bracken past a house to join Sygun's driveway. Just before the road bends to cross a bridge over the river, take the signposted path ahead to gates. Follow the path for ½ mile to the footbridge just before Llyn Dinas.

WALK 19
SYGUN

DESCRIPTION The 2¾ mile walk, combines well with a visit to 19thC Sygun underground copper mine. After a long steady climb from Llyn Dinas up to to top of Grib Ddu (918 feet/280 metres) the route descends via Bwlch-y-Sygyn to Sygun, then follows the river back to Llyn Dinas. Allow about 2 hours..

START Roadside car park on A498 near Llyn Dinas SH 612494 or at entrance to Sygun SH 605490.

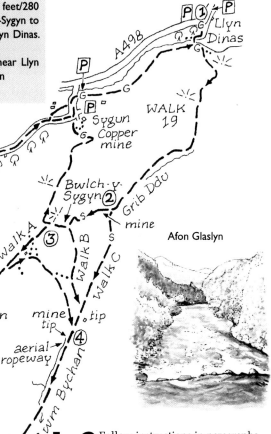

Afon Glaslyn

1-2 Follow instructions in paragraphs 1 & 2 of Walk 18.

3 Continue on the stony path down the steep rhododendron-covered hillside, later passing the entrance to Sygun mine, then a side path leading to Sygun museum, shop and café, to reach a minor road. Keep ahead and follow the road past the entrance to Sygun and its car park. Just before it bends to cross a bridge over the river, take the signposted path ahead to gates. Follow the path for ½ mile to the footbridge just before Llyn Dinas.

CWM BYCHAN & CWM NANMOR

DESCRIPTION An 8 mile walk of great variety, featuring contrasting upland valleys, a beautiful lake, woodland, mining relics and extensive views. The route climbs steadily up Cwm Bychan which was mined for copper from the late 18thC until 1930, and contained an ore-processing plant. It passes the remains of an aerial ropeway, reaching a height of 951 ft/290 metres, before descending to continue alongside Llyn Dinas. After rising across open country, it follows a quiet upland road, then paths through the attractive wooded Nanmor valley, before returning to Nantmor. Allow about 5 hours.

START National Trust Aberglaslyn car park, Nantmor SH 597462 or roadside car park near Llyn Dinas SH 612494.

DIRECTIONS The pay & display car park lies off the A4085, near Nantmor.
For Llyn Dinas start see Walk 18.

I Go through a small gate by the ticket machine and toilets. Turn RIGHT signposted Cwm Bychan to pass under the railway bridge. Go past picnic tables and up to a cross path. Follow it RIGHT up through woodland and on to a small gate. The path briefly accompanies the stream, then rises steadily up Cwm Bychan, later passing aerial ropeway pylons and a former copper mine. Keep ahead, rising steadily past a ruin and waste tip on your right, later becoming more enclosed by heather/boulder covered ridges. Cross a ladder-stile at the highest point – *with views of Snowdon, Moel Siabod, and Cnicht.* Follow the path LEFT to a finger post at the top of Grib Ddu. Turn RIGHT down the stony path signposted to Llyn Dinas. The path begins a long steady descent, later levelling out, before a final steeper descent to Llyn Dinas.

2 Turn RIGHT along the lakeside path, over a stream and on to a ladder-stile. Take the waymarked path up through heather, bracken then trees, and down to a ladder-stile just beyond a ruin. Continue down the path, over a stream and on by the fence to cross a ladder-stile over it. Follow the path up across the wooded slope, soon taking its right fork to pass above a ruin. After a ladder-stile the path rises to a viewpoint, then descends briefly before rising steadily through bracken. After briefly levelling out – *with a view across to Snowdon and Y Lliwedd* – the path continues up to a ladder-stile then up to another.

3 The path rises through rhododendrons and passes a cottage to a ladder-stile. Turn RIGHT through a wall gap, then follow the path LEFT beside the wall and on across open ground to a ladder-stile/gate at the corner of a small wood. The path now crosses a small rise ahead, then descends to follow a wall over a track and up across higher ground ahead and down to cross a ladder-stile over it. Turn LEFT and follow the path near the wall down and up onto the small ridge ahead. Turn LEFT along its top, then angle RIGHT down past a telegraph pole. At a ladder-stile continue beside the wall to a gate by Blaen Nant onto a minor road. Follow it RIGHT along the attrac-

tive upland valley, past a cottage, then old spoil heaps, now accompanied by the infant Nanmor river. The valley gradually becomes more enclosed.

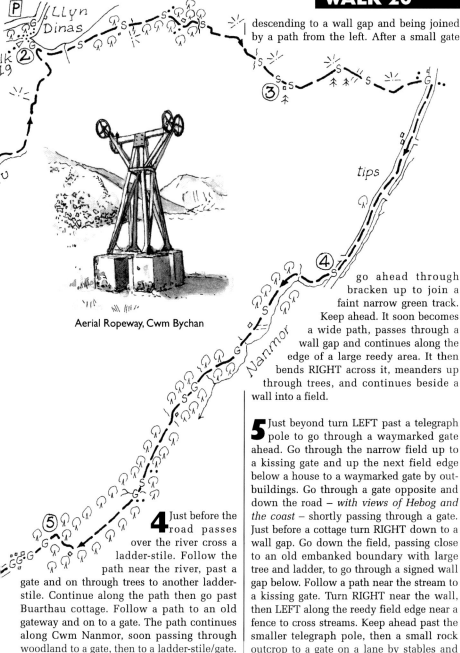

Aerial Ropeway, Cwm Bychan

descending to a wall gap and being joined by a path from the left. After a small gate

4 go ahead through bracken up to join a faint narrow green track. Keep ahead. It soon becomes a wide path, passes through a wall gap and continues along the edge of a large reedy area. It then bends RIGHT across it, meanders up through trees, and continues beside a wall into a field.

5 Just beyond turn LEFT past a telegraph pole to go through a waymarked gate ahead. Go through the narrow field up to a kissing gate and up the next field edge below a house to a waymarked gate by outbuildings. Go through a gate opposite and down the road – *with views of Hebog and the coast* – shortly passing through a gate. Just before a cottage turn RIGHT down to a wall gap. Go down the field, passing close to an old embanked boundary with large tree and ladder, to go through a signed wall gap below. Follow a path near the stream to a kissing gate. Turn RIGHT near the wall, then LEFT along the reedy field edge near a fence to cross streams. Keep ahead past the smaller telegraph pole, then a small rock outcrop to a gate on a lane by stables and Cilfynydd. Go down the lane to a road by a chapel. Follow it RIGHT down through Nantmor, over the railway line, to the A4085. Turn RIGHT back to the car park.

4 Just before the road passes over the river cross a ladder-stile. Follow the path near the river, past a gate and on through trees to another ladderstile. Continue along the path then go past Buarthau cottage. Follow a path to an old gateway and on to a gate. The path continues along Cwm Nanmor, soon passing through woodland to a gate, then to a ladder-stile/gate. The path now rises through the trees, levels out then passes behind a cottage and crosses a stream. After passing through two wall-gaps, the path rises through woodland, soon

WALK 21

GELERT'S GRAVE

DESCRIPTION A 1¼ mile riverside walk, on level paths suitable for wheelchairs & pushchairs, featuring the grave and sculpture of the legendary dog. Allow about 1 hour.
START Beddgelert SH 590481.

1 From the village bridge, take the riverside lane signposted to Gelert's grave/toilets. Just before the footbridge, go through a gate and follow the wide riverside path south. Shortly, turn RIGHT to follow another path to Gelert's grave and on to a ruin containing a bronze sculpture of the dog.

2 Turn LEFT along another path back to the river. Go through a gate by a small building and continue south alongside the river, later crossing a footbridge over it, by the railway bridge, to return along the other side.

WALK 22

BRYN DDU

DESCRIPTION A 3¼ mile walk via Gelert's Grave, following a waymarked National Trust path up to Bryn Ddu tower (603 feet/184 metres) offering panoramic views, then descending through Coed Aberglaslyn to the A498. It returns through the beautiful wooded Aberglaslyn Pass, near the Welsh Highland Railway, initially via the rocky Fisherman's Path above the river – *care needed*. Allow about 2 hours.
START Beddgelert SH 590481.

1 Follow the instructions in paragraph **1** of Walk 21.

2 Go through a small gate ahead and follow the National Trust path, then track, to the A498. Take the National Trust path opposite up to cross the railway line. Follow the path to a gate, then along the next field edge to a ladder-stile. The waymarked path passes old workings, rises to a small gate, then climbs to Bryn Ddu tower and a ladder-stile, before descending through

Coed Aberglaslyn to a small gate at point 4. Turn LEFT down to the A498. Follow it LEFT to the junction. *Until the early 19thC, Aberglaslyn was a small tidal port boasting copper exporting and boat building.* Go over the bridge and through a kissing gate on the left. Now follow the Fisherman's Path above the river. Later, after crossing the railway, continue along the river's right bank to Beddgelert.

WALK 23

PEN Y GAER

DESCRIPTION A 4¼ mile (**A**) or 4 mile (**B**) walk for experienced hill walkers, exploring wild upland Open Access land south of Beddgelert, reaching a height of 886 feet/270 metres. After visiting Pen y Gaer, an old Welsh castle, it descends into Coed Aberglaslyn. Walk A returns on a National Trust waymarked path via Bryn Ddu tower, requiring initial further climbing, but rewarded by fine views. Walk B offers a riverside return via Aberglaslyn Pass. Avoid in poor visibility. Allow about 3 hours.
START Beddgelert SH 590481.

1 Follow the A498 Porthmadog road through the village past the Tourist Information Centre. Take the signposted bridleway up past the Royal Goat Hotel. On the bend go along a short stony track, then LEFT up a signposted path between houses to cross a bridge over the railway. Follow a path ahead to an old gateway and on to follow a wall to a ladder-stile/gate. Go up the path, soon taking its right fork, and on up to an old gateway ahead. Continue up to pass a waymarked fence corner below a telegraph pole, then a gate, after which the path rises steadily to a gate onto a track. Go through the gate opposite and up the long reedy field on intermittent paths, past a waymarker post, to gates in its left-hand corner between forest sections into Open Access land.

2 Keep ahead through bracken above the forest wall. After about 50 yards, angle RIGHT to follow a slight sunken path up the hillside, then the left-hand side of a wider reedy one up to a large boulder. Cross an old wall just above. A few yards higher turn LEFT up a reedy cross-path. After it quickly fades head up to nearby small rock outcrops. Just beyond turn LEFT to follow an improving path across the slope to a viewpoint, looking down into Aberglaslyn valley. Bear RIGHT and follow the path south along the part reedy narrow shelf, then up to a small gate in a wall – *with a view to Cnicht.* The path briefly accompanies an old wall. Soon it descends towards Cnicht and crosses another old wall. A fainter path angles down LEFT and improves as it crosses a small ridge beneath another wall. After crossing a stream, briefly go down beside it, then turn RIGHT down to a small gateway between stone sheepfolds linked to a large crag.

3 Just beyond angle LEFT down the reedy/ bracken slope to cross a stream below, with a ruin ahead. Turn RIGHT through bracken a few yards, then angle LEFT up towards trees, with Cnicht beyond, to go through a gap in an old wall. Follow a narrow track LEFT down to pass a remote upland cottage and outbuildings. Follow its old access track – *with Pen y Gaer ahead* – down to pass through a gate. As it angles right go along a path on the left. After a few yards climb up through Pen y Gaer 's northern entrance to enjoy panoramic mountain views. Return down the slope and turn RIGHT along the path to cross a nearby wall. Descend LEFT to go through a wall gap by a small ruin. Turn RIGHT along a short walled path through bracken to a wall gap. Just beyond turn LEFT down beside the wall. Continue down, soon passing a fence corner, then follow an intermittent path across reedy ground to an old wall near the stream and forest. Follow a good path, initially above the stream, down to a stile into Coed Aberglaslyn. Descend a meandering old walled stony path, then a cross-path to cross a footbridge over a gorge. (For **Walk B** continue down to the A498 and follow instructions from 6th sentence in par. 2 of Walk 22.)

4 For **Walk A** go through a small gate ahead and follow the waymarked National Trust path up through the trees

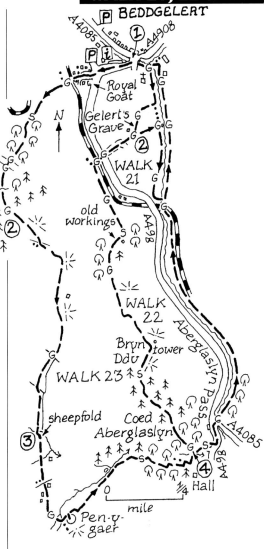

to eventually emerge from the forest via a ladder-stile. Follow the path up to a viewpoint, then to a tower on Bryn Ddu. After a short climb the path begins a long steady descent to a small gate. Continue down past old workings to a ladder-stile, then along the next field edge to a gate. Follow the path to cross the railway line onto the A498. Go along the track opposite. When it bends right, keep ahead to a small gate, then follow a path past Gelert's grave to the village.

BWLCH-Y-DDWY-ELOR

DESCRIPTION A 5 mile walk featuring open forest, a hidden upland lake, the impressive remains of a remote 19thC slate quarry, an historic pass and good views of Snowdon. The route follows tracks and paths through Beddgelert Forest via Llyn Llywelyn to emerge into open country below Y Gyrn. After passing through the former Prince of Wales slate quarry at the head of Cwm Pennant, the route follows an old coffin route across Bwlch-y-Ddwy-elor at about 1312 ft/400 metres, then returns on bridleways through the forest. If timed right there are good views of Welsh Highland steam trains at the beginning and end. Allow about 3 hours. Another option is a simple walk to picnic at Llyn Llywelyn and lake circuit on forestry tracks

START Beddgelert Forest car park SH 573503.

DIRECTIONS From Beddgelert take the A4085 towards Caernarfon. After 2 miles turn left at Pont Cae'r Gors entrance to Beddgelert Forest. Follow the stony track, parallel with the railway for 600 metres down to a signposted car park off to the right.

I Return to the main track, then follow it RIGHT down past a wooden chalet, then a house. Take the next track on the right to cross an old stone bridge over the river (Pont Rhydceffylau). Follow the track ahead up to cross the railway line – *with a good view of Moel Hebog.* Go past post 57 ahead and up a path through trees, then turn RIGHT along a former forestry track, now little more than a wide stony path. After crossing a stream it rises steadily – *with a good view of Snowdon.* At a crossroad of stony tracks continue up the one ahead. At the next crossroad keep ahead to reach a Mountain Bike information board by Llyn Llywelyn. Turn LEFT along a stony path past nearby lakeside picnic tables – *a good place to stop to enjoy the lake's tranquility* – then across the dam and over a footbridge. Turn RIGHT up a track above the side of the lake and on through the forest.

2 About 75 yards after crossing a low bridge over a stream, just beyond post 11 at a large turning area, look for a path leading left through the trees. After an inauspicious start a good path passes through a gap in a wall, briefly accompanies it, then rises near the forest edge and continues up through conifers. When it levels out you meet a cross-path at post 33. Follow it RIGHT, soon descending to cross a stream to reach an old forestry track beyond. Follow it LEFT for 100 yards, then at post 34 turn RIGHT to follow a waymarked path up through trees to a stile into open country. Just ahead, cross the wall on your left and follow a path alongside it down and along the edge of a marshy area – *with the Nantlle ridge ahead.* At the wall corner, where it rises, turn LEFT and follow the path around the mid-slopes of Y Gyrn – *soon with views along Cwm Pennant, with a small reservoir below.*

3 After passing a small building, you reach a good viewpoint overlooking the former Prince of Wales slate quarry (1873-86), with its network of tramways and inclines. *The quarry had a water-powered mill, barracks and weighbridge and operated underground, pit and gallery workings. Despite considerable investment it was a commercial failure.* Follow the path down into the quarry, passing to the left of a large deep hole. Midway, follow a path bending left, then turn RIGHT past a nearby small ruin. Immediately turn RIGHT behind it and follow a path up to a small waste tip above where the stream emerges from a rock face. Just above, turn sharp LEFT along an old tramway, then past old buildings. At their end do a sharp U-turn RIGHT to follow a path beneath tips and up an old incline, past a large supporting wall beneath another level of buildings. Continue ahead along a shelf, past small buildings, and on past a nearby large quarry hole, following a path up through reeds to the end of a tramway coming in from the left. Follow a good path ahead up the part reedy valley, shortly angling left to a small gate.

4 Follow the path across Bwlch-y-Ddwy-elor (Pass of the Two Biers) – *an ancient route between Rhyd Ddu and Cwm Pennant used for carrying the dead by bier for burial.*

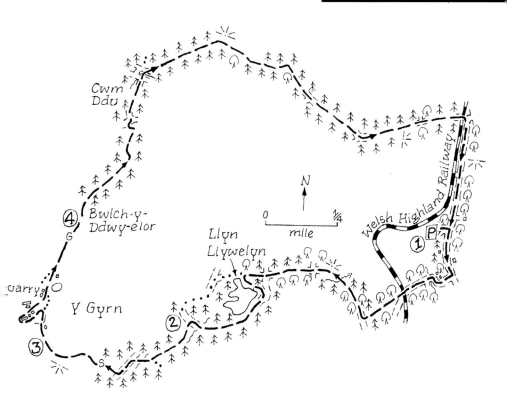

Prince of Wales quarry

It is said that at the pass a coffin would be met by men with a second bier and the coffin transferred onto it for the final part of the journey – hence its name! It must have been a sad and arduous journey for grieving families, especially during the winter. The path then descends through the forest to eventually reach a forestry track. Turn RIGHT. At the nearby junction, turn LEFT on the waymarked bridleway. Follow the track to another junction at Cwm Ddu. Turn LEFT across the stream, then immediately turn RIGHT to follow the stony bridleway through trees to a another nearby track. Turn RIGHT along the track (another bridleway), shortly descending to pass through an open area – *with good mountain views.* At a track junction keep ahead. At the next turn LEFT, soon descending past a side track to cross the railway line to reach the forest entrance. Return along the track to the start.

BWLCH CWM LLAN

DESCRIPTION A 5 mile linear upland walk, linked to Sherpa bus services, from Rhyd-Ddu to Nant Gwynant, crossing a high mountain pass between Snowdon and Yr Aran, offering extensive mountain views. The route follows a good track – initially the Rhyd-Ddu path to Snowdon – up to pass through old slate quarries to reach Bwlch Cwm Llan (1672 ft/510 metres). After descending into the dramatic setting of Cwm Llan it then follows the Watkin Path down to Pont Bethania. Allow about 3½ hours. It combines well with Walk 26.

START Rhyd-Ddu car park SH 525571.

DIRECTIONS From Pont Bethania car park (See Walk 13) take the S97 bus (Betws-y-Coed – Porthmadog) to Beddgelert, then the S4 bus (Caernarfon) or Welsh Highland train to Rhyd-Du car park.

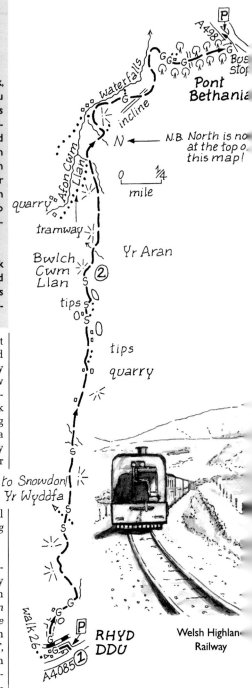

1 Enter the car park and follow the road past toilets. At the far end take the signposted path across the railway line. Go up the stony track, soon taking its right fork. The track now rises steadily for over 1½ miles, then passes through the lower slate quarry. The track then narrows and becomes a slate path rising beneath tips and by ruined buildings, then a small incline. It levels out at the upper quarry area. Go past a ladder-stile to cross another further along the fence beneath tips. Follow the path through a wall gap, past a small lake and alongside the fence to a ladder-stile. Keep ahead to cross a collapsed wall at the top of Bwlch Cwm Llan – *overlooking Cwm Llan, with a new view of Snowdon.*

2 After an initial short steep descent, follow the path's right fork on a long steady descent across the mid-slopes of Yr Aran into Cwm Llan – *with views of the Snowdon ridges, Y Lliwedd, and South Snowdon Slate Quarry below.* Later, the path follows a stream down to the old tramway. Follow it RIGHT, then take a path down into the valley to join the Watkin Path on a long steady descent, initially past waterfalls, and later through woodland, to Pont Bethania.

WALK 26

SNOWDON RANGER TO RHYD-DDU

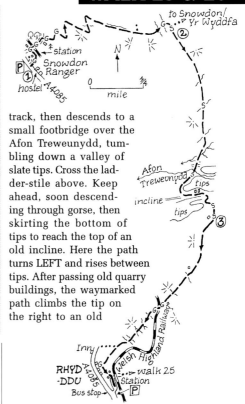

DESCRIPTION A 4 mile linear walk, connecting two popular Snowdon starting points, combined with a short ride on the Welsh Highland Railway, or local bus. The route follows the Snowdon Ranger Path to a height of 1246 feet/380 metres, then takes a very well way-marked link path on a long steady descent via an attractive gorge and old slate quarry back to Rhyd-Ddu. Allow about 3 hours.

START Snowdon Ranger SH 565551.

DIRECTIONS From Rhyd-Ddu car park take the Snowdon Sherpa S4 bus (Beddgelert – Caernarfon) or Welsh Highland Railway to Snowdon Ranger stop/halt. (Tel: Traveline Cymru: 0871 200 22 33)

The narrow gauge Welsh Highland Railway opened in 1923 connecting Caernarfon with Porthmadog via a standard gauge transfer at Dinas. The goods and passenger railway was abandoned in 1937, but is currently being re-instated, and due to be completed by 2009.

I From the bus stop take a signposted path opposite. (From the end of the railway platform follow a path beside the line.) Cross the railway line and go up the track. Just beyond the house (*note the waterwheel*), turn RIGHT up through a gate and follow the path up to another gate. It now zig-zags up the hillside, later angling across the slope. It then levels out – *with a view ahead of Snowdon* – passes a signposted bridleway to Llanberis, and bends round to a gate by a stream. After a further 50 yards, leave the Snowdon Ranger path to cross a ladder-stile on the right.

2 Follow a path on a steady descent, guided by waymarkers and finger posts, to cross a footbridge over a stream, then a ladder-stile by another stream. The path continues down to cross further streams and a slate track, then descends to a small footbridge over the Afon Treweunydd, tumbling down a valley of slate tips. Cross the ladder-stile above. Keep ahead, soon descending through gorse, then skirting the bottom of tips to reach the top of an old incline. Here the path turns LEFT and rises between tips. After passing old quarry buildings, the waymarked path climbs the tip on the right to an old tramway, then bears RIGHT and LEFT and descends across the waste to a ladder-stile. Continue to another ladder-stile ahead.

3 After a few yards, angle down the slope past waymark posts and over a stream. At a waymarker post by a small crag, bear LEFT across the slope to go through an old wall gap by a small tree. Go through another wall gap ahead, over a stream and across a wettish area. The path now descends, crosses a footbridge, goes through a wall gap and continues down towards Rhyd-Ddu. After crossing the railway line follow the way-marked path across a series of small sleeper bridges, then follow a good path beneath high ground. At a waymarked path junction, take the left fork to eventually go through a kissing gate by houses at Rhyd-Ddu. Turn LEFT up a track, passing between houses, and on to the car park.

29

MOEL EILIO

DESCRIPTION A 8 mile mountain walk featuring one of the finest grassy ridges in Snowdonia, offering extensive views of mountains, coast and Snowdon Mountain Railway. The route rises in stages above Llanberis, then climbs steadily to Moel Eilio (2381 ft/726 metres) and continues along the undulating ridge to Foel Goch. It then descends and returns along an attractive valley and near a river. Allow about 5½ hours. *For experienced hill walkers. Avoid in poor visibility. The bridleway crossing the Afon Goch is expected to be reopened by the early summer of 2014 after the installation of a new bridge*

START Snowdon Mountain Railway, Llanberis SH 584597.

DIRECTIONS The station is at the eastern end of the village.

*T*he Snowdon Mountain Railway was built in 1896, with the 5 miles of track laid in just 72 working days. It works on a rack and pinion system, with the engines, some steam, pushing thousands of people to the summit each year.

From the Snowdon Mountain Railway entrance follow the road towards the nearby Royal Victoria Hotel then turn RIGHT along Victoria Terrace. Shortly, take a road on the right across the river, under the railway bridge, past a children's play area and side road then turn LEFT across a cattle grid and follow the signposted footpath (waterfall) up a lane. Just past a cottage, go through a kissing gate on your left for a view of the waterfall. Continue up the lane past a track, then on the bend go through a kissing gate ahead. Go up the field edge to a waymarked path junction by a wall corner/kissing gate. Go across the wide path and on up to a kissing gate by a stream. Follow the stream up to another kissing gate then the wall up to a road by Hafod Uchaf. Go up the road to a gate onto a track.

2 Turn RIGHT to a ladder-stile/gate and follow the delightful bridleway to cross

the Afon Goch and on to a minor road. Follow the road up past a ruin, then a green track up to a ladder-stile. The track rises steadily across the hillside. *A new hydroelectric power scheme is being developed in former slate quarries north of the track.* Shortly after a gate, where the track levels out, take a wide path angling LEFT up beneath power cables. It continues up the hillside, shortly joining another stonier path for a climb up the northern slope of Moel Eilio, later alongside a fence to a ladder-stile, then another on the summit of Moel Eilio. Go to two small stone shelters ahead to enjoy great all-round views.

3 Return to the fence and follow it down to a ladder-stile – *with a view of Llyn Dwythwch below.* Continue down near the fence, soon joining a wide path which levels out, then rises to a ladder-stile. Now follow a faint path across the broad flat summit, soon descending and passing the end of a wall. The path now rises to pass above the head of Cwm Dwythwch, then goes along the small ridge of Foel Gron, before descending the broad steep grassy ridge. It then rises again up Foel Goch to a fence corner and continues alongside the fence to cross a ladder-stile ahead. Head half-RIGHT, then angle down the steep slope to a path junction at Bwlch Maesgwm. Bear LEFT on a stony path. It descends the western edge of Maesgwm valley, later levelling out to eventually accompany a wall to a gate. The path gently descends, later passing above ruins then a cottage. Go down its stony access track, through a gateway and on for a further 20 yards.

4 Go through a gate below, head down to a nearby ladder-stile. Follow the path across the reedy field to a stile, and on across the next to cross a bridge over the Afon Arddu. Turn LEFT up a boulder path

30

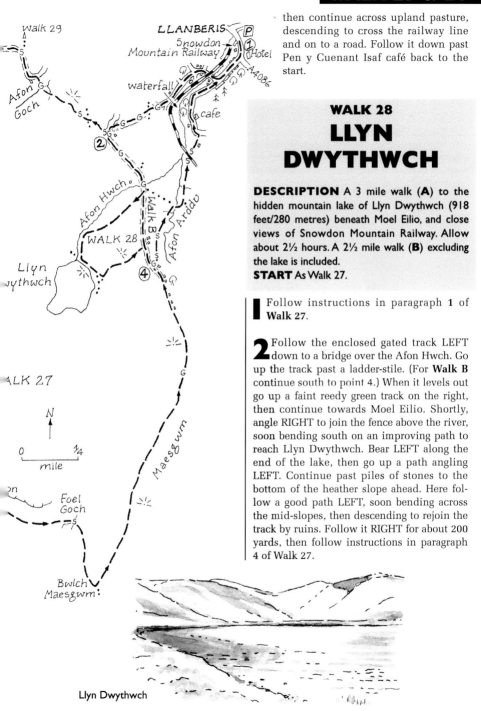

then continue across upland pasture, descending to cross the railway line and on to a road. Follow it down past Pen y Cuenant Isaf café back to the start.

WALK 28
LLYN DWYTHWCH

DESCRIPTION A 3 mile walk (**A**) to the hidden mountain lake of Llyn Dwythwch (918 feet/280 metres) beneath Moel Eilio, and close views of Snowdon Mountain Railway. Allow about 2½ hours. A 2½ mile walk (**B**) excluding the lake is included.
START As Walk 27.

I Follow instructions in paragraph **1** of Walk 27.

2 Follow the enclosed gated track LEFT down to a bridge over the Afon Hwch. Go up the track past a ladder-stile. (For **Walk B** continue south to point 4.) When it levels out go up a faint reedy green track on the right, then continue towards Moel Eilio. Shortly, angle RIGHT to join the fence above the river, soon bending south on an improving path to reach Llyn Dwythwch. Bear LEFT along the end of the lake, then go up a path angling LEFT. Continue past piles of stones to the bottom of the heather slope ahead. Here follow a good path LEFT, soon bending across the mid-slopes, then descending to rejoin the track by ruins. Follow it RIGHT for about 200 yards, then follow instructions in paragraph 4 of Walk 27.

Llyn Dwythwch

31

CEUNANT MAWR WATERFALL

DESCRIPTION A 2½ mile walk **(A)** exploring the countryside above Llanberis, featuring a waterfall and a prominent hill (1050 ft/320 metres), the site of an Iron Age fort, offering panoramic views. Allow about 2 hours. A bridleway crossing the Afon Goch is expected to be re-opened by the early summer of 2014, after installation of a new bridge. An alternative 1½ mile walk **(B)** is included.
START Dolbadaran Hotel, High Street, Llanberis SH 579601

I Head south east, then at Snowdon Garage turn RIGHT along a road past the church. Soon after it bends left take a signposted path through a gate on the right up to a kissing gate. Follow the path past a cottage then up through trees to another kissing gate and on to briefly join a track. Take a path angling RIGHT from a telegraph pole, then go up a lane. Just past a cottage go through a kissing gate on the left over the railway line for a view of the waterfall. Continue up the lane past a track to a kissing gate ahead on the bend. Go up the field edge to a waymarked path junction by a wall corner/kissing gate. Go across the wide path and on up to a kissing gate by a stream. Follow the stream up to another kissing gate then the wall up to a road by Hafod Uchaf. (For **Walk B** follow it back down to Llanberis.) Go up the road to a gate onto a track.

2 Turn RIGHT to a ladder-stile/gate and follow the delightful bridleway to cross the Afon Goch and on to a minor road. Follow it up past a ruin, then continue up a green track. At a ladder-stile follow the wall RIGHT to a kissing gate. Go up to the top of the narrow hill for extensive views. Return to the kissing gate, then follow the path east down to another kissing gate and on down the hillside to the road. Follow it down to Llanberis.

LLYN PADARN

DESCRIPTION A delightful 5 mile way-marked white trail around Llyn Padarn. After visiting the former quarry hospital, it rises through the ancient woodland of Coed Dinorwig past seasonal Padarn cafe (01286 871979 for opening times), then descends to the lake end. Its lakeside return includes the Lon Las Peris former railway track. Allow about 3 hours. The trail can easily be started from various lakeside car parks, or the village.
START Slate Museum car park, Llanberis SH 585603.
DIRECTIONS The museum lies at the eastern end of Llyn Padarn.

The National Slate Museum occupies an old Victorian quarry workshops, that once provided repair and maintenance for the Dinorwig quarry. It provides a fascinating insight into the slate industry. It is open throughout the year and is free.

Llyn Padarn and nearby Llyn Peris were named after early Celtic saints, who founded Christian churches in the area. Llyn Padarn, a designated SSSI, is home to the Arctic Char, a rare fish that has survived here since the Ice Age. It forms part of the Padarn Country Park established in 1969 – the first in Wales. The Llanberis Lake Railway runs on a narrow gauge track originally built in 1842 to transport slates to Port Dinorwic. It closed in 1961, but re-opened for passengers to Penllyn in 1972, then extended into Llanberis in 2003. The steam locomotives date from 1889-1922.

Llanberis developed as a new quarrying village, but later became a popular Victorian tourist resort, attracted by guided climbs up Snowdon. Its popularity increased after 1869 with the opening of a branch railway line from Caernarfon, then the building of the Snowdon Mountain Railway in 1896.

I At the far corner of the car park, follow the signed Quarry Hospital and Padarn Lake walks, then multi-coloured trail up

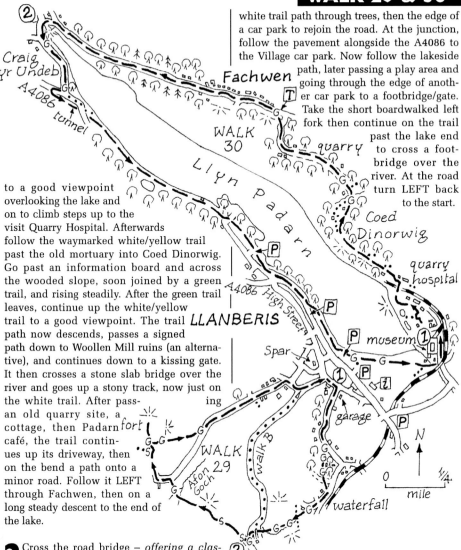

white trail path through trees, then the edge of a car park to rejoin the road. At the junction, follow the pavement alongside the A4086 to the Village car park. Now follow the lakeside path, later passing a play area and going through the edge of another car park to a footbridge/gate. Take the short boardwalked left fork then continue on the trail past the lake end to cross a footbridge over the river. At the road turn LEFT back to the start.

to a good viewpoint overlooking the lake and on to climb steps up to the visit Quarry Hospital. Afterwards follow the waymarked white/yellow trail past the old mortuary into Coed Dinorwig. Go past an information board and across the wooded slope, soon joined by a green trail, and rising steadily. After the green trail leaves, continue up the white/yellow trail to a good viewpoint. The trail **LLANBERIS** path now descends, passes a signed path down to Woollen Mill ruins (an alternative), and continues down to a kissing gate. It then crosses a stone slab bridge over the river and goes up a stony track, now just on the white trail. After passing an old quarry site, a cottage, then Padarn café, the trail continues up its driveway, then on the bend a path onto a minor road. Follow it LEFT through Fachwen, then on a long steady descent to the end of the lake.

2 Cross the road bridge – *offering a classic view along the lake* – then turn LEFT along the old road, now part of the Lon Las Peris. Follow it past Crag yr Undeb (Union Rock) – *associated with the formation of the North Wales Quarrymen's Union in 1874* – to the A4086. The trail continues ahead briefly along the pavement. A better choice is to follow the Lon Las Peris to cross the road and on through a short railway tunnel. Follow the tree-lined former Caernarfon-Llanberis railway line near Llyn Padarn to a road by toilets. Turn LEFT, then RIGHT to follow the

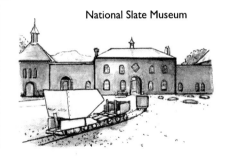

National Slate Museum

WALK 31

VIVIAN QUARRY & COED DINORWIG

DESCRIPTION A 3¾ mile (**A**) or 1¾ mile (**B**) walk using using waymarked trails to explore the local quarrying heritage and Coed Dinorwig. After visiting the former quarry hospital, the route passes a working incline and climbs the steep wooded slope with hidden quarry terraces. It then heads NW through the ancient oak woodland and splits. Walk A continues to Dinorwig. Walk B heads east to pass above Vivian quarry. Both combine for a delightful final descent past Anglesey Barracks. Allow about 2½ hours. An interesting 1 mile (**C**) walk is also included.

START Slate Museum car park, Llanberis SH 585603.

DIRECTIONS The museum lies at the eastern end of Llyn Padarn.

I At the far corner of the car park, follow the signed Quarry Hospital and Padarn Lake walks, then multi-coloured trail up to a good viewpoint overlooking the lake and on to climb steps up to visit the Quarry Hospital. Go along its access road, soon descending. At post 3, take a parallel yellow/blue trail path on the left past a working incline and old buildings to a viewpoint overlooking water-filled Vivian quarry. (For **Walk C** continue down the path and along the road, then take a trail path on the right to descend a short incline to the diving centre building to visit the quarry pool.) Return 10 yards to take the blue Vivian stepped trail up the oak covered slope. At the third terrace of old quarry buildings the blue trail is now diverted along it past a winding house. It then joins the yellow trail and continues along a former tramway, shortly descending to be joined by the green trail, before rising. When the green trail descends continue up the yellow/blue trail to a path T-junction by a footprint post. (For **Walk B**, turn right and follow the yellow/blue trail up to leave Coed Dinorwig by a ladder-stile, through a kissing gate and on up through bracken, then along a track. Just before a gate the trail descends through trees, passes above Vivian quarry, then descend in stages to point 3.)

2 Turn LEFT and follow the yellow trail on a long steady descent past an information board and side path to a kissing gate, where the yellow trail descends left. Follow the path ahead to a footbridge, then kissing gate. Go up a track to a lane. Follow it RIGHT past cottages. When it bends right turn LEFT along a signposted enclosed gated path into a field. Follow the path to Ty Newydd farm and up its access track to a road by an old chapel. Take the signposted path almost opposite up to a wider road in Dinorwig. Follow it RIGHT to a lay-by and a slate monument. Continue along the no through road to White Peris, then go down a stony track past cottages. At a driveway to houses follow the narrow track ahead to a Padarn Trails sign.

3 Follow the blue/yellow trail down through trees, past nearby Anglesey barracks – *which housed workers from Anglesey until 1948* – to a footbridge by a winding house. Continue down a delightful narrow walled path – *enjoying good lake views* –– then through trees to join the road. At the nearby junction turn RIGHT to return to the Museum.

WALK 32

DINORWIC QUARRY

DESCRIPTION A 5¼ mile (**A**) or 4½ mile (**B**) heritage walk, featuring the massive Dinorwic slate quarry. After an initial steep but delightful climb across the slate waste and oak covered hillside to Anglesey Barracks, Walk A continues up to the edge of Dinorwig then heads SE to enter the quarry. Walk B makes a more direct climb via inclines into the quarry. After a long steady meandering descent through the quarry to Llyn Peris, the route returns alongside the lake for a visit to Dolbadarn castle. Allow about 3 hours.

START Dolbadarn car park, Llanberis SH 585599, or lay-by on the A4086 SH 598587.

DIRECTIONS The car park is on the left on the road signposted to Padarn Country Park/ Slate Museum.

34

*D*inorwic slate quar-
ry, carved out of the
mountainside, developed
from small-scale 18thC
workings to become one
of the largest in the world
during the 19thC to meet
increasing demand for
roofing slate, employ-
ing 3000 men at its
peak in 1870. Slate
from here was
exported world-
wide. After a long
steady decline, the
quarry finally closed in
1969. Hidden deep inside
the mountain is Dinorwic
Pump Storage Power Station,
which pumps water from
Llyn Peris up to the
storage reservoir of
Marchlyn Mawr.

2 Follow the blue trail to a
great viewpoint. Return to
go through the larger kissing
gate and follow the wide
fenced track across the
vast quarry, later meandering down the slate waste
covered hillside to Llyn
Peris and on to reach the
A4086. Follow the pave-

| Continue along the
road past the side
road leading to the Slate
Museum, then take a
signposted path on the
left. Follow the blue/yellow
trail up through trees, then a delightful narrow walled path – *offering great
lake views* – to a small footbridge by an
old winding house. The trail continues up
through the wood. Shortly divert RIGHT to
nearby Anglesey barracks – *providing basic
accommodation for workers from Anglesey
until 1948.* (For **Walk B** continue between
the barracks, then follow the blue trail up
a railed incline to a winding house, and on
to climb another incline to a kissing gate at
point 3.) Continue up through the wood.
At a Padarn trails sign, leave the rising trail
and go along a narrow green track, then
up an access track past cottages to join a
road. Follow it to a good viewpoint with
seats. Turn RIGHT into a large lay-by to a
kissing gate in its corner. Follow the signposted Slate Trails along a narrow stony
track to enter Dinorwic quarry. Go past
quarry buildings to a pair of kissing gates.
Turn RIGHT.

ment alongside the lake. Later, take a track
down towards Dolbadarn castle, then follow a path through trees round to visit the
massive circular keep – *part of the castle
built by Llywelyn the Great in the early
13thC. In 1282 it was seized by the English,
then abandoned.* From a small building
take a path down through the wood to the
road.

WALK 33

NANT FFRANCON

DESCRIPTION A 5½ mile walk, with extensive views, exploring a classic glacial valley, used by Telford to build his coaching route through the mountains. The route climbs through woodland and across Open Access land on the eastern side of the valley, reaching a height of 1377 ft/420 metres. After a delightful long steady descent, it returns along the valley on an old road, then a section of the Lon Las Ogwen recreational path beneath Penrhyn quarry. Allow about 3½ hours.

START Lay-by on A5 south of Bethesda SH 627654.

DIRECTIONS The lay-by is near the entrance to Ogwen Bank Holiday Park, about ½ mile south of the A5/B4409 junction.

Just beyond the driveway to Ogwen Bank cross to a small gateway opposite into the Braich Melyn wood. Follow a path up through the trees, over a stony track, and on up through the wood to a small gate. At a large forestry turning area beyond turn RIGHT and follow an initially wide, then narrow stony path up through mixed woodland to a small gate into Open Access land – *with a good view across to Penrhyn quarry and along Nant Ffrancon*. The path now rises steadily above the wall. Shortly, it bends sharp LEFT up through gorse. When the ground levels out about 100 yards before a forest corner, turn RIGHT to follow a path up the hillside, passing about 12 yards to the left of a stone sheepfold. About 30 yards higher turn RIGHT along a fainter path then head towards the wall ahead. Follow the wall eastwards up through gorse and reeds along the edge of Nant Ffrancon, shortly descending then rising again before contouring across rough upland pasture.

2 At the far top corner of a forest cross a stream then another further ahead. Follow a third stream up alongside the wall, then cross it to a small iron gate. Go through reeds to a ladder-stile/gate ahead into National Trust owned land. Follow the way-

marked path LEFT to another ladder-stile. Continue along the wide path past a post. After another the path narrows and descends towards the valley. After about 15 yards, just before a large rock and waymarker post, turn RIGHT down a line of stones, then LEFT down a wide path beneath the waymarker post. The path continues down beside a reedy stream and crosses a bridge over it. The reedy path gently descends across the steep hillside to a ladder-stile/gate, after which the delightful wide green path makes a long steady descent to another ladder-stile/gate. Continue down the reedy path.

3 After about 120 yards, turn sharp RIGHT down another reedy path to a small gate in the wall corner. Follow the path down the garden edge of a nearby house, over its driveway and down to a small gate onto the A5. Cross the road with care to a kissing gate opposite. Go down the edge of a long field and across a footbridge over the Afon Ogwen. Cross a low stone stile then go across three fields to join a minor road by Maes Caradog farm. Follow the road west along the valley past a house. On the bend go through the gate ahead and along the Lon Las Ogwen stony path, later undulating and meandering beneath large slate quarry waste tips of Penrhyn quarry – *which developed under the ownership of the Pennant family since the late 18thC, into the world's largest opencast slate quarry, with slate going by rail to Port Penrhyn, Bangor for shipping around the world*. After joining the river, it passes through gates and descends above small falls to further gates. Turn RIGHT through another gate and go across the bridge over the river to the entrance to Ogwen Bank, then follow its driveway up to the A5.

WALK 34

AFON OGWEN

DESCRIPTION A 3 mile walk featuring the Afon Ogwen, Penrhyn quarry and the Lon Las Ogwen recreational path. Allow about 2 hours.

START As Walk 33.

1 Go down the driveway to Ogwen Bank, then across the stone bridge over the river to a gate onto the Lon Las Ogwen. Turn LEFT through nearby gates and follow the stony track up past small falls and through other gates. The undulating and meandering track continues south beneath slate quarry waste tips of Penrhyn quarry (see par. 3 of Walk 33 for information), then along the expansive valley. At a minor road follow it LEFT.

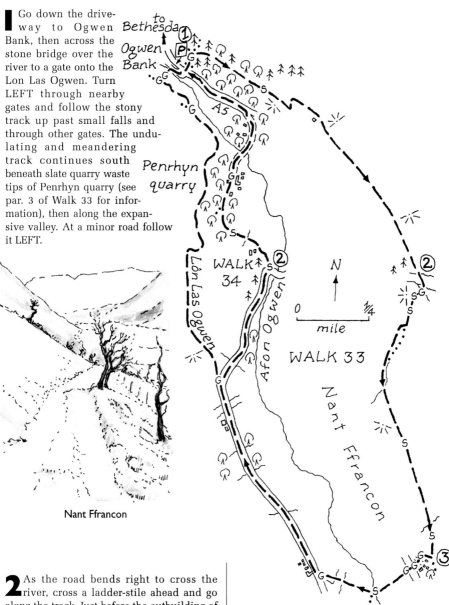

Nant Ffrancon

2 As the road bends right to cross the river, cross a ladder-stile ahead and go along the track. Just before the outbuilding of nearby cottages angle RIGHT down through reeds and bracken past a telegraph pole to the wall ahead. Follow it LEFT to a ladder-stile. Continue near the wall, soon rising. After it levels out continue through bracken to join a path running just above the wall, soon descending past outbuildings towards a farm. Follow the wall past a gate and a small building above the main complex to go through a small gate in the wall. Follow the farm's access track across the river and on to the A5. Follow the pavement back to the start.

37

LLYN OGWEN

DESCRIPTION A 3 mile low-level walk around Llyn Ogwen, one of the shallowest lakes in Snowdonia enclosed by mountains, featuring delightful Ogwen waterfall and a new Visitor Centre and cafe at its western end. Its follows a roadside pavement along its southern side and a waymarked National Trust path, rocky and wet in places, along its northern side, offering great lake and mountain views without the crowds. Allow about 2¼ hours
START Car park on the A5 by Llyn Ogwen SH 656602.
DIRECTIONS Travelling west along the A5 from Capel Curig, when you reach Llyn Ogwen, park in the third National Trust Glyderau car park on the left – the last before Ogwen Cottage.

I Follow the pavement opposite east above Llyn Ogwen – *with Tryfan towering above.* Go past the end of the lake then turn LEFT on a signposted path along a track over the river, then past Glan Dena into Open Access land. Continue along the stony track. Just before a gate at the farm entrance, take the waymarked National Trust path on the right up to cross a ladder-stile in the wall. At a waymarker post just beyond a nearby stream, ignore the rising red stony path and take another path on the left down through bracken and reeds to another post. Follow the waymarked path above the farm, then down to cross two forks of the Afon Lloer and a stile. Continue with the path, guided by regular white-topped posts across the reedy, stone covered terrain – *with great views of Llyn Ogwen, Tryfan, Y Garn, and Pen-yr Ole Wen up to your right* – to another stile.

2 After about 100 yards, the path splits. Keep with the lower waymarked left fork, over a stream, across a rock slab, and on past further posts, passing under electricity cables, then following them across the hillside. The path passes through a wall gap, then under the cables and heads towards Llyn Ogwen, continuing down to a ladder-stile near the lake. The path soon passes an old pill box and continues beside the lake to its end, then passes through an area of large boulders to join the river, then reach the A5. *Note the remains of an old arched stone bridge beneath the road bridge.* First go through a small gate opposite to a crag overlooking Rhaeadr Ogwen, then follow the pavement up to a side road just before Ogwen Cottage Outdoor Centre. Follow it to the nearby Visitor Centre and café. Return to follow the pavement alongside the lake back to the start.

LLYN IDWAL

DESCRIPTION A 3¼ mile walk (**A**) combining a short section alongside Llyn Ogwen with a circuit of Llyn Idwal, lying at about 1200 ft/365 metres within the dramatic glacial valley of Cwm Idwal – the first National Nature Reserve in Wales – whose rock faces support important rare plants. Allow about 2½ hours. Included is a 3 mile (**B**) walk with a more direct finish across open ground and a shorter 2 mile walk (**C**). Walks A/C can be shortened by starting from the Snowdonia National Park pay & display car park near the Visitor Centre at SH 649604.
START As Walk 35.

I Follow the pavement west alongside the lake, then take the side road by Ogwen Cottage Outdoor Centre to the nearby Visitor Centre, café and toilets. Go up the wide stony path past the near end of the Centre. After a few yards turn RIGHT up a side path between rock faces to a ladder-stile. Follow the path up through the gully, soon climbing out of its right side to a stile. The path continues across open ground, soon rising steadily – *with views of Tryfan, the Glyders and Cwm Idwal/Y Garn ahead* – then crosses level ground to a stile in a fence – *with a view of Llyn Idwal.* Follow the path ahead and after about 50 yards, when it bends right up towards Y Garn, follow another path ahead down towards the lake, over a cross-path, to reach the stony shore. (For **Walk C** turn left alongside the lake, then

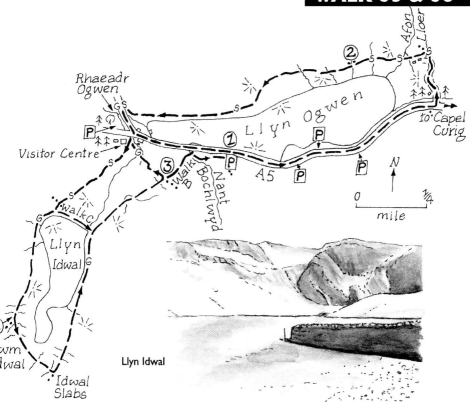

Llyn Idwal

follow a path to a footbridge over the lake's outlet to join the return path beyond.) Turn RIGHT along the shore to a gate in the wall and follow the path alongside the lake, soon rising and continuing towards the head of the valley.

2 Later, just before the main path begins to rise towards Twll Ddu (Devil's Kitchen) ahead – *a narrow cleft in the mountain* – take a stony path on the left down to cross two streams. Continue across level ground beyond the end of the lake towards Idwal Slabs – *a famous rock climbing site* – then follow a meandering stone path up to join a cross-path beneath the Slabs. Follow it LEFT back along the eastern side of Cwm Idwal, past the lake and through a gate. After passing the footbridge over the lake's outlet, continue with the wide stony path, shortly descending – *with a view of Llyn Ogwen ahead.*

3 Just after it bends left you have a choice. For **Walk A** continue down the main path to a footbridge over the river and on down to join your outward route near the Visitor Centre. (For **Walk B**, take a stony path on the right. After a few yards, turn left along a green path down towards Llyn Ogwen. When it splits, follow the path left down the hillside, then descend past a wettish area to a ladder-stile by the road (an alternative return option). Cross the bridge over the river. Go past another ladder-stile and National Trust sign. Follow a path onto the small ridge, then up towards Tryfan, parallel with the nearby river. After about 80 yards, at the sharp end of a rocky ridge, turn left along another path down to the fence overlooking the road, then the wall to a ladder-stile into the car park.)

PRONUNCIATION

Welsh	English equivalent
c	always hard, as in cat
ch	as in the Scottish word loch
dd	as th in then
f	as f in of
ff	as ff in off
g	always hard as in got
ll	no real equivalent. It is like 'th' in then, but with an 'L' sound added to it, giving 'thlan' for the pronunciation of the Welsh 'Llan'.

In Welsh the accent usually falls on the last-but-one syllable of a word.

KEY TO THE MAPS

- ➝ Walk route and direction
- ══ Metalled road
- ─ ─ ─ Unsurfaced road
- •••• Footpath/route adjoining walk route
- ∿∿➔ River/stream
- ♣☿ Trees
- ▬■▬ Railway
- **G** Gate
- **S** Stile
- **F.B.** Footbridge
- ↘╎↙ Viewpoint
- Ⓟ Parking
- Ⓣ Telephone

Useful contacts

Beddgelert TIC: 01766 890615
Llanberis TIC: 01286 870765
National Trust: www.nationaltrust.org.uk
Snowdonia Society: www.snowdonia-society.org.uk
Snowdonia National Park Authority:
   www.eryri-npa.gov.uk
Sherpa bus timetables: gwynedd.gov.uk
Met Office Mountain Weather:
   www.metoffice.gov.uk (0870 900 0100)

THE COUNTRYSIDE CODE

- Be safe – plan ahead and follow any signs
- Leave gates and property as you find them
- Protect plants and animals, and take your litter home
- Keep dogs under close control
- Consider other people

Open Access
Some routes cross areas of land where walkers have the legal right of access under The CRoW Act 2000 introduced in May 2005. Access can be subject to restrictions and closure for land management or safety reasons for up to 28 days a year. Details from: www.naturalresourceswales.gov.uk. Please respect any notices.

About the author, David Berry

David is an experienced walker with a love of the countryside and an interest in local history. He is the author of a series of walks guidebooks covering North Wales, where he has lived and worked for many years. He has been a freelance writer for Walking Wales magazine, worked as a Rights of Way surveyor across North Wales and been a member of his Local Access Forum. For more information visit:
   www.davidberrywalks.co.uk

Published by **Kittiwake Books Limited**
3 Glantwymyn Village Workshops, Glantwymyn, Machynlleth, Montgomeryshire SY20 8LY

© Text & map research: David Berry 2014
© Maps & illustrations: Kittiwake 2014
Drawings by Morag Perrott
Cover photos: *Main* – Llyn Dinas, Walk 16. *Inset* – Dolbadarn Castle, Llanberis, Walk 32. David Berry

Care has been taken to be accurate. However neither the author nor the publisher can accept responsibility for any errors which may appear, or their consequences. If you are in any doubt about access, check before you proceed.

Printed by Mixam, UK.

ISBN: **978 1 908748 17 1**